The Kind of Old Man I Want to Be

A PARADIGM FOR 65 AND BEYOND

Jack Chalk

Antioch Publications
United States of America

Copyright © 2016 by Jack Chalk

Published 2016 by Antioch Publications, USA

All rights reserved. No part of this publication may be reproduced, distributed or transmitted in any form or by any means, including photocopying, recording, or other electronic or mechanical methods, without the prior written permission of the publisher, except in the case of brief quotations embodied in critical reviews and certain other noncommercial uses permitted by copyright law.

ISBN:
978-0-9967929-3-6 - Print
978-0-9967929-4-3 - Mobi
978-0-9967929-5-0 - ePub

Scripture quotations, unless otherwise indicated, are taken from THE HOLY BIBLE, NEW INTERNATIONAL VERSION®, NIV® Copyright © 1973, 1978, 1984, 2011 by Biblica, Inc.® Used by permission. All rights reserved worldwide.

Cover image by Tommaso Lizzul © 123RF.com

*To Ann, my beautiful wife.
Thank you for putting up with this old man.*

Contents

Preliminaries

Old as Being Rather Than Doing   1

Fun to Live With   19

Laconic   31

Carpe diem   47

Life: The Rest of the Story   81

Life: The End of the Story   97

Life: The Meaning of the Story   129

Epilogue   149

Preface

My purpose in writing this book is to create a DIM (do it myself) guide to old age in hopes that you, my reader, will DIY. In it I will describe the kind of old man I want to be (DIM) hoping that you will think about and start working on the kind of old person you want to be (DIY) when your time comes if it hasn't already.

The thesis of this book is that being old is more about being than it is about doing. We should start being the kind of old person we want to be as early in life as possible, surely by middle age. You are not going to change your character and personality at a retirement party. You will continue to be the type of person you are now until you die unless you make a conscious effort to change some things. I am starting later in life than I should have, but it is too late to start any sooner.

You will find a lot of quotes throughout the book. That is because I am not clever myself but I can quote people who are. In the words of the sixteenth-century French philosopher, Michel de Montaigne, "I do not speak the minds of others except to speak my own mind better." In other words, I quote others only in order to better express myself.

I recommend two other books. One is *Treatise on Friendship and Old Age* written by Marcus Tullius Cicero in 44 BC. The other is *Learn to Grow Old* by Dr. Paul Tournier. If you take away nothing else from Tournier's book besides the encouragement to start preparing for old age long before I did, it will be worth your time to read it.

May you find my book entertaining, encouraging and edifying, but not something you are enduring as you grow older reading it. Rejoice, if you are not getting older, you are dead.

"Age is just a number—
the sum of which
took me years to add up."
—Yours truly, CPA

[1]
Old as Being Rather than Doing

> "If I had known that this was the kind of
> old man I was going to be,
> I would have started sooner."
> —Anon. (A famous old person!)

YOU AND I ARE WITNESSING something that is unprecedented in the history of the United States. The number of people getting old is at record rates. And I am helping. Yes, I am one of the 76 million babies born after World War II during the years 1946 to 1964. We are called the Baby Boomers. We are the largest generation of older people ever assembled in the US and we started turning 65 in 2011. And I, being born in 1946, was in the first class of Boomers to turn 65. But when I had my 65th birthday I was not alone. On my birthday 9,999 other Boomers had their 65th birthday. That's right, 10,000 Baby Boomers per day are turning 65 and they are joining the 45 million people who are already there. Folks, that is a lot of old folks.

Look at it this way. There are a whole flock of people age 50 and above who are being herded toward the gate marked "65" and 10,000 per day are going through it. What does that gate lead to? For the minority it will lead to a pasture of green grass, financial security, comfort and years of good health. For others, it will open on to a rocky pasture with an oasis only now and then to sustain them. And for others, what lies beyond the 65 gate is a desert of poor relations, lack of finances, and poor health—a life full of emptiness. Statistics show that not many of us are prepared for what is on the other side of the gate. Many do not have a plan, a map or a blueprint for being 65 and beyond. Wise counsel for contentment in old age is needed.

How many old people are content with being old? We are human beings and not human doings so maybe contentment hinges more on being (the kind of person we are) than on doing (what we fill our time with). Many old people are finding things to kill time while they are waiting for time to kill them. That is not the kind of old man I want to be.

Old people pass through the gate and enter the pasture. On the other side of the pasture, opposite the gate, is a door—death's door. We don't know how long we get to stay in the pasture, but we do know that everyone who enters the gate will leave by the door. Are we prepared for that door to open for us? Are we prepared to die? I certainly want to be the kind of old man who is content to live and content to die. That is real contentment. I will have more to say about contentment throughout the book. I just want you to know that we can learn a lesson about contentment from Henry Ford, the founder of the Ford Motor Company. He retired a millionaire but he was content to live and to die never having owned a Cadillac.

If you have a question, somebody has already asked it, done the research to obtain the answer, and has posted the answer on the Internet. I was wondering at what age people consider themselves to be the most content. Sure enough, *Psychology Today* published some research done on the subject in the US. The winner was 41 as the age of contentment. In the

UK, the Daily Mail reports the age of contentment to be slightly lower at 37. The majority responded that most of their life goals had been completed at that age. Why do I bring it up and why it is important to this work? I am concerned about older people being content in their old age. The *Psychology Today* article went on to say, "But once people hit 65, most people think their ideal age is behind them. For those over 65, the age of contentment is 59." My purpose for this book is to convince people that the age of contentment does not have to be ahead of or behind you; it can be your age today and everyday of your life.

What would make a person content in their old age? The answer is obvious. People who have family close by, financial security, and good health are the most content. Remember that we Baby Boomers broke all the rules and we are paying the price as we enter old age. The divorce rate for this generation is the highest in US history. Families are shattered and scattered. Consumer credit has overextended us to where the markets cannot support us and the value of retirement funds has taken a severe hit in recent years. Good health can go in a second, and we are less likely to have it the older we get. The obvious basis for contentment in old age is not the reality for most of us old people.

The above is reflected in the suicide rate for those 65 and older. The suicide rate for those 65 and older is 20% higher than for the general population. The suicide rate for white males 65 and over is almost three times the national average, and for those over 85 the rate is almost four times the national average. What do we make of all this? I would think that the older we get the less content we are. I have come up with a paradigm (to use a late-twentieth- century word) for being 65 and beyond that works for me. It helps me to be content regardless of my circumstances and I believe it will do the same for others.

Being old is not a new thing. I am blessed and grateful to have a brother several years older than I am to show me it is doable. But it is a new thing for me. I have done the research and formulated this paradigm for being old. I invite you to read my mind as you read this book about the kind of old man I want to be. Hopefully, it will help some of you through the gate and out the door.

Let me stop already and ask if you read the Preface to this book. Many people skip the Preface. If you did, I ask that you go back and read it as it gives my purpose for writing the book and really sets the tone for it. Thanks a lot!

Back when I had my 65th birthday I realized that the majority of the people in the world would consider me an old man. I am in the minority (i.e., in denial), so I got to thinking about what kind of old man I wanted to be when I got to be one. I did not want it to just happen. I did not want to just morph into an old man, so I decided to be proactive and choose the kind of old man I wanted to be and then to take steps to be that kind of person. I don't want to be old, but it is the only way I know to have a long life.

As I am writing this, my wife and I are about halfway between 65 and 70 years old. We still have good health and are able to go and do; however, we are finding it takes us longer to get over going and doing. I write about the kind of old man I want to be with my wife in mind. She will have to put up with whatever kind of old man I am and she deserves the best, so, I will try to be the best old man I can.

I also write with my mother in mind. She died in her early 80's after a few years in a nursing home. Her experience there gave me the opportunity to observe older people at their most vulnerable. There were some who were a joy to be around and some that the attendants were not paid enough to be around. What was the difference?

This was about 20 years ago and I started thinking then that a place like this could very well be my future. Some, like my mother, were not able to walk; some were not able to talk. Could I handle this if it was me? When I turned 65 I realized that the possibilities have become probabilities and I better get busy preparing myself for being an old man. What kind of old man do I want to be?

Now, I don't claim to know how the milk got in the coconut, but I am reasonably intelligent and I should be able to figure this old man thing out. I don't want to be like many old men who, like I said before, look for things to do to kill time while time is killing them. I have learned to look thoughtful even when I am not thinking, but I have also done a lot of actual thinking about the kind of old man I want to be.

Being a Christian, I started thinking about what kind of old man Jesus would have been if he had been crucified at 83 instead of 33 years of age. Would he have been different from 65 to 83 than he was from 30 to 33? Probably not, since He lived a sinless life from 30 to 33. I, on the other hand, lived a very selfish life from 30 to 33 and want to live just the opposite from 65 to 83.

In thinking about what is coming, the breakdown of the body comes to mind first. Someone has described old age as when former classmates are so grey, wrinkled and bald they don't recognize you. There is some fact in that truth. I can do all I can to maintain my body and use God's gifts of doctors when sickness comes. But eventually things that I cannot control will happen in my body. I will be less active and more dependent. How am I to handle that? The way I handle it will be determined by the kind of old man I am.

There are some things that I cannot do anything about and there are some things that I can. So, I will concentrate on the things I can be proactive about. One is my character or personality. I do not want to be a grumbling, complaining old man. I want to be an old man who is positive and not negative. I want to have the temperament that makes for happiness and contentment for me and those around me.

The first step I took in my effort to determine and then become the kind of old man I want to be was to see what help was available. Perhaps someone has already taken this approach to getting old and has written a book about it. I found many books on aging and growing old and they all had two things in common.

Psychologists like to write books and many have written books on the aging process. So, I started there. Having studied psychology, and having taught psychology at college level, I knew that the purpose of secular psychology is to help people cope with whatever situation they are dealing with. The coping advice comes in the form of various things a person can do given the limited control they have over people and circumstances.

Coping and doing are the two things in common all the books I encountered on growing old focused on. They focus on helping a person cope with getting old and they focus on what to do in order to cope with getting old. I do not want to just cope. To cope has a passive aspect meaning to tolerate or endure; and it has an active form meaning to deal with and attempt to overcome problems and difficulties associated with whatever the person is coping with (noisy neighbors, pain, growing old, etc.). Coping involves doing and doing is what most people lose the ability to do as they grow old. I want to concentrate on being rather than doing—the kind of old man I want to be, rather than what I want to try to do different because I am old. I don't want to just cope; I want to be proactive, to manage myself as I get older.

Among the books I looked at when researching what has already been written about growing old was *Lastingness: The Creative Art of Old Age* by Nicholas Delbanco. Expecting it to tell how to turn growing old into an art form, I found out it was about artists who produced some of their greatest works in their old age. It is a good book, but it is about doing—doing artsy things late in life that most of us could not do early in life.

I did learn something interesting about the artist Claude Monet. He is considered to be the first of the Impressionist painters. Without going into the details of what Impressionism tries to portray about its subject, it can be said that Impressionistic paintings are characterized by slightly blurred rather than sharp outlines of the subject. It is an effort to capture the impression of reflected light off the subject. Now, what I learned was that Monet, the pioneer of this art form, had cataracts. Looking at an Impressionist painting is how someone with cataracts would see a normal painting. Was Monet just painting things as he saw them through eyes with cataracts? Or, if his cataracts came later in life (which in fact they did), did he see things with blurred lines through his cataracts the way he had already been painting them? Was his mind already trained to see things that way so that cataracts were not a problem for him? Of course, this is just the musing of an old man that has nothing to do with this book I am writing.

Another book that looked hopeful in turning growing old into an art form is *The Art of Growing Old: Aging with Grace* by Marie de Hennezel, a French clinical psychologist. In her book she mixes philosophy, spirituality and psychology focusing on one's attitude toward growing old. She takes the position that refusing to age and go with the flow, so to speak, is actually what makes a person become old. And I thought it was accumulating a lot of years that makes me become old! She offers an interesting concept to growing old with grace, the concept of non-action. She is talking about doing nothing so that you can become aware of what is around you. In non-action, one's perception and senses are heightened. Unless you fall asleep, as many old people do. Non-action seems to come naturally to old people. Maybe I should put down this pencil (yes, I'm writing the old fashion way) and embrace non-action. Anyway, hers is a well written book and has received very good reviews. It would be a great help to those who want to cope well with growing old. However, I don't want to cope with growing old, I want to manage it.

Again, another book in my library written by a psychologist is *Time on Our Side: Growing in Wisdom, Not Growing Old* by Dorothy Rowe. The approach taken by Dr. Rowe in this book is guided by her basic premise that we all fear, even have a horror, of growing old. She writes about these fears, but my impression was that the fears are her own. In this book the author comes across as cynical and believing in nothing permanent or of lasting value. The chapter titles reveal a lot about the author:

> The Fearful Passage of Time
> Fearing to Grow Old
> Youth and Age: A Mutual Antipathy
> Laying Eggs and Hatching Vultures
> From Absolute Truths to Uncertain Wisdom
> From Absolute Time to Created Time
> Time and Timelessness

In reading this book I got the impression that the author has some deep issues unresolved in her life (but I am only human and I could be wrong). She is presenting these issues, which are somewhat revealed in the chapter titles, as the reality of all people who are growing older. Even if I was just looking for help in coping with growing old, this book would tend to depress me.

I sure do not want to write a depressing book about getting old. Maybe I don't need to concentrate on the things I cannot control and focus on the kind of person I am. That I can control and change if necessary. The way I view life is this: being directs doing. If I am a happy person I will do fun things. If I am a responsible person I will do the responsible thing even if it is unpleasant. Psychologists do not concentrate on being, but on doing. When a person does something positive that they think will help their situation, they immediately feel better. Feelings are dictating doing. But those feelings are short-lived and something else must be done to feel good again. If you are the right kind of person, then feelings will not be controlled by what you do but by the kind of person you are. I have done a lot of thinking about the kind of old man I want to "be."

One book I consulted that appeared to be more positive is *Growing Old: A Journey of Self-Discovery* by Danielle Quinodoz. The author is a Swiss psychoanalyst who wrote the book from the perspective of her own advanced age. She reminds us of the fact that we are aging every minute in her opening to Chapter 1: "I have become even older in just the time it took me to write one sentence! You took the time to read it, so that you are older, too." (Please don't take that personally as you take the time to read my book.) The basic premise of her book is about an older person reconstructing their own internal life-history so that looking back on one's life it has coherence. Our life tells a story and we need to be comfortable with it as we look back on it. If we are not comfortable with it, we need to reconstruct it so that we are. The older we get, the more losses we accumulate, and in the midst of those losses we must not lose ourselves.

The book presents a self-absorbed approach to being old, suggesting that we need to reconstruct our life-history so that the path it follows leads to where we want to end up. That is a good trick if you can do it. We all know that you can only reconstruct history in your mind. But you can change your life-path today so that you will end up where you want to be. More about this in Chapter 7.

Now, I want to admit that I also have in my library the *Oxford Specialist Handbook of Old Age Psychiatry*. I will let the foreword speak for the text: "Despite major strides in understanding the pathogenesis of the major psychiatric syndromes of late life, the available treatments help only a fraction of patients." As a reasonably well-educated older adult with reasonable reasoning ability, the following kind of language from that same handbook scares me and makes me seek a higher Source than man in my old age:

> *In late-life depression, attention to comorbid cognitive abnormalities began to clarify its pathogenetic mechanisms. Executive dysfunction is common in depression of old adults. Depressed elders with executive dysfunction have a clinical presentation resembling medial frontal lobe syndrome, poor or slow short-term response to antidepressants, and chronic or relapsing long-term course.*

Is the non-action of Marie de Hennezel the same as executive dysfunction? These books that I have mentioned are good books in their field and are commendable to those seeking help in coping with getting old. That is not my goal. It is my belief that the kind of old person I am will determine my well-being in old age and that coping with the particular circumstances I find myself in will be a natural by-product of being the right kind of person.

Not all the books I researched are professional works of psychologists who take growing old seriously. Some authors take a humorous approach to growing old while offering some advice for coping with being old. I will mention these books by title and author and will be quoting from some of them from time to time in this work. There are many on the market and these are the ones I bought:

> *You're Old, I'm Old ... Get Used to It!* by Virginia Ironside
> *Old Age and How to Survive It* by Edward Enfield
> *Old Age Comes at a Bad Time* by Eliakim Katz
> *I Don't Know What Old Is, But Old Is Older Than Me* by Sherwood Eliot Wirt
> *Old Git Wit* by Richard Benson
> *If You're Over the Hill You Oughta' Be Goin' Faster* by Carl Malz

Carl Malz, the author of the last book listed, was a pastor and then missionary serving as president of Southern Asia Bible College and then founder of the Middle East School of Theology. His wife, Betty, was an acquaintance of my wife. Carl and Betty died in 2012. Having known about them for years, I was excited that Carl had written a book on getting old. It turned out the "You Oughta' Be Goin' Faster" refers to doing things at a more rapid pace because your time is running out. Although it focuses on doing, it is doing with the assumption that you are the right kind of person. He writes: "Age only accentuates what you are, it amplifies your mindset and the condition of your spirit."

"What you are," "your mindset" and "your spirit" as they apply to me is the focus of my attention as I write this book on the kind of old man I want to be.

In thinking through the kind of old man I want to be, I decided to analyze character traits and write down certain ones that I want to be true or present in me. If I am going to be positive and not negative, lovable and not hateful, what attributes need to describe me? The following is what I came up with as my paradigm for the kind of old man I want to be.

If I am going to be a loveable old man, I need to be a loving old man, one that loves first. That means that, to me, other people are more important than I am. That is a tough one right off for us older people who, as we get older, tend to focus on ourselves and our needs and circumstances. That means I must have strong affection for, hold dear and cherish (not in the romantic sense) other people above myself. That's hard to do when your bones ache and the air conditioning in the place is too cold for you. But loving I must be.

To be loving and to show love I must be joyful. If I am a joy to be around, I must have joy as an integral part of my character. That means this joy is not dependent on circumstance. Joy does not come from dwelling on ourselves, our problems, our hurts, and our past. Nor does it come from a happy-go-lucky attitude, as if nothing mattered. Joy is not a spontaneous response to some temporary pleasure. Joy is not mere happiness in present circumstances that are good. Good circumstances can make us happy because happiness depends on happenings. Joy is not dependent upon what happens. Therefore, joy is not incompatible with grief and sorrow. The opposite of joy is not sorrow as one would expect. The opposite of joy is hopelessness and despair. As long as I maintain my joy I will never be hopeless or despairing. For me, I find this joy in knowing who I am as a Christian. All I hope for and hope to be is, for me, given to me in Christ, both now and in eternity. I want to be an old man who is a joy to be around.

To be the kind of old man people love to be around I need to be patient. That means patient with the man who is depriving a village somewhere of an idiot. That means being patient with those who think they drank at the fountain of knowledge when it is obvious that they only gargled. Patience is a character trait that is passive and should be easy for an old man who becomes more passive as the years roll on. It requires no physical action to be patient with people. It does involve an element of self-sacrifice when difficult people provoke you. It involves exercising understanding of people and circumstances and it requires you to have the capacity to calmly endure difficult people and circumstances. To be patient requires us to exercise self-restraint when being provoked. That means being able to control your temper when most people would have lost theirs. The element of self-sacrifice comes in because being patient requires you to absorb injury without resentment, indignation or the desire to retaliate. That is a tall order for an old man of average height.

You cannot be patient with people unless you are quick to forgive them. Forgiveness wipes the slate clean and relieves you of keeping records of wrongs perpetrated against you. Wiping the slate clean is the "forget" part of "forgive and forget." Forgetting should be easy for an old person. If we keep mental records of hurts felt by what people say or do to us, any little present offense will open the book and lay all the past offences before you. How can you be patient with a person who has this record? You cannot! Therefore, to be patient with people without being willing to forgive people is impossible. The older I get, the more I appreciate company. I do not want someone to stay away from me just because they may have hurt me in the past. Patience and forgiveness keep the door open for relationships. That is very important to me as an old man.

When thinking about the kind of old man I want to be, the word "kind" naturally comes to mind. I want to be a kind old man. Being kind (showing kindness) is a character trait that is active. It requires a deliberate act of the will to do something positive to help a certain person or a certain situation. Kindness requires a sweet disposition and goodness of heart. Being kind involves being gracious, pleasant, hospitable and benevolent. Acts of kindness are done without regard to the worth or merit of the one who receives it and in spite of what that person deserves. I want to be a nice old man but I would rather be a kind old man. To be nice is to have a pleasant disposition (saying "please" and "thank you"), but to be kind requires that I do something good for someone else when I am not required to. It will take some effort to be kind and I will try.

To be kind and to have a nice disposition does not mean that you cannot tell people the truth when you are asked. It does involve separating facts from opinions. That seems to be a problem with many old men. Speaking the truth in a kindly manner should be a trait we all have, regardless of age. But for an older man to speak what he believes to be the truth in a harsh way will quickly get him branded as a grouchy, bitter old man. Man! I want to avoid that reputation.

One of the things I like in other people, and one I want other people to associate with me, is the quality of being faithful. To be faithful means keeping commitments in relationships. It is fidelity which makes one true to his promise and faithful to his task. It also means being a safe place to deposit a secret. How many old people like to gossip? Being faithful involves steadfastness, dedication, loyalty and stability. A faithful old man is dependable and worthy of trust. How many faithful friends does one have in a lifetime? In my old age, I want to be such a friend.

Another trait I want to have as an old man is the quality of gentleness. So many people have been beat up and hurt in their dealings with other people. A gentle word can be healing to their souls. I want to be one people come to for a gentle word spoken in a gentle manner. That requires a tenderness of feelings and a disposition that is even-tempered, tranquil and unpretentious. It is going to be hard but I want to be known as a gentle person.

For me to be proactive in exhibiting these character traits and qualities covered so far, and to avoid the ones I don't want to have, is going to require the positive trait of self-control. Without self-control there can be no victory over tongue and temper or over a spirit that is judgmental, critical and unforgiving. Self-control is a rational restraint of natural impulses, especially in older people who tend to give in readily to natural impulses. How many old men do you know who have a calm and dispassionate approach to life, having mastered personal desires and passions? Usually, the opposite is true in old men. I want to be the kind of old man who has self-control, exercising restraint and discipline over my personal behavior. Am I dreaming?

Of course, in thinking about the kind of old man I want to be I must consider the negative aspect—the kind of old man I do not want to be. I certainly do not want to be prideful. I do have a beautiful wife (who likes to say she is 39 and holding; someone once asked me how old she would be if she let go, but I didn't say), reasonably good health and some wealthy relatives, but I did not have anything to do with any of these things. And I certainly have nothing to boast about. Pride is taking credit for one's own achievements or one's connections with someone who has achieved. Boasting is bragging about those achievements or connections in such a way that could cause others to be jealous of those achievements or connections. It results from an excessively high opinion of oneself producing feelings of self-satisfaction.

Old men like to brag about what they used to do or who they used to know. (I shook hands and had a personal conversation with the great golf legend, Arnold Palmer, in a bar in Pensacola, Florida in the 1970's; but I do not want to brag about it, you know what I mean?) I do not want to be prideful of what I have or have done, nor do I want to be jealous of what others have or have done. Pride and jealousy are two things I do not want in my life as I consider the kind of old man I want to be.

Rude people of any age are people to be avoided. I do not want to be the kind of old man who people avoid so I do not want to be rude. Rude means to be impolite or even insulting. It can also mean to act improperly, dishonorably or indecently. The five senses tend to diminish as we get older. I do not want to be an old man with a diminished sense of propriety, honor or decency. I do not want that to describe me, therefore I do not want to be rude in my old age.

Most of what I have written about so far can be accomplished in my remainder if I am the kind of old man who is not selfish or self-seeking. That means that I should not care too much about me and not enough about others. It means being an old man who honors and prefers others before myself. That is really going to be hard to do when my joints ache or the music is too loud. But do it I must, if I am going to be the kind of old man I want to be.

I guess the bottom line is that I want to be an old man who is at peace and content whatever my circumstances are. My mother's final years were spent confined to a wheelchair in a nursing home. She still owned a home complete with furniture and keepsakes she had had for many years. Yet, she was content where she was. The fact that she had Alzheimer's, which allowed her to live a totally different life in her mind not knowing where she really was, helped some. In fact, on one visit when she was 80 years old she told me that she had made a decision—she was going to quit her job and go back to school. Of course, the family supported her in that decision. But still, I want to be an old man who has that kind of peace and contentment (without the Alzheimer's).

It is easy for old people to sit around lamenting effects, and forgetting causes altogether. Growing old is something I do not want to think about, but it is something I cannot forget. I must plan for it by, first, being the kind of person I want to be, and then by doing what that kind of old man does. In the words of Will Rogers, I want to endeavor to live so that when I die even the undertaker will be sorry. To have good character traits and not bad ones is one thing—to live them out is another. Now I will share with you how I want to live out my remainder being the kind of old man I want to be.

[2]

Fun to Live With

> "There is little difference in people, but that little difference makes a big difference. The little difference is attitude. The big difference is whether it is positive or negative."
> — W. Clement Stone

FOR THE SAKE OF MY WIFE and those who may share my company in a nursing home someday, I want to be an old man who is fun to live with. I don't mean that I want to be a silly old man, but an old man who is fun to be with 24 hours a day. To live with me and for it be fun, I need the character traits that I have already mentioned. It also makes sense for me to have a sense of humor. Henry Ward Beecher, American social reformer and clergyman, said, "A person without a sense of humor is like a wagon without springs. It's jolted by every pebble on the road." Old men do not like to be jolted so I need to find humor in life's jolts.

Like Mr. Stone said, I certainly need a positive attitude. Now that I have some years behind me, I realize that I started this life with nothing and I still have most of it. So why shouldn't I be positive? Having the attitude of looking for the positives in midst of the negatives is actually a fun way to be. I don't have to worry about making a comeback because I have not been anywhere. It is not hard for me to meet expenses because they are everywhere. Maintaining a positive attitude will keep me from being a grumpy old man and I would not like for my wife or my future co-residents to have to live with such a man.

My wife and I are living in Spain as I am writing this. The Spanish word for fun is *diversión*. It is the same as our English word diversion. A diversion is a temporary detour from a normal route or course. It can also mean a temporary pleasant or amusing pastime or activity. In order for me to be fun to live with, the fun needs to be normal and not temporary. It must be the normal course and not a diversion and it must be a way of life.

Now, I have to admit that I have not always been fun to live with. There was a time, not too many years ago, when we were travelling by car while in the US on a temporary visit. It was raining and I was tired of driving on the crowded interstate highway, so we got off at an exit, found a restaurant and had a nice lunch. We sat in a booth next to the window watching it rain. When we had finished eating it had stopped raining, so I paid the bill and we got back on the interstate and away we went. After we had been travelling about 20 minutes, my wife said, "Oh No!" I said, "What?" She said: "I left my glasses on the table at the restaurant!" I felt the steam start rising.

Before we were called to be missionaries I worked for 25 years as a Certified Public Accountant in the United States. That profession charges by the hour, so that time means money. We had been travelling for 20 minutes and it was about 15 miles to the next exit where we could turn around to go back to the restaurant. This whole thing was going to cause us to lose at least an hour of travelling time. But, now that I am old, the association of money with time has changed since now I have more time than money. Given the cost of eyeglasses these days, it was not a question of spending the time to go back to get them.

I was not at my most fun to live with and as the steam within me rose, the words flowed. "You are always forgetting things!" "If your head was not attached you would forget it!" "If your shoes were not laced to your feet you would leave them too!" On and on I went. When we finally got back to the restaurant, it had started raining again. I pulled up to the front door and as my wife was getting out in the rain I said, "Honey, would you get my umbrella while you are in there?" Needless to say, she failed to see the fun in that, and only because she is a better person than I am, the umbrella was not wrapped around my head.

If you ask me, I am a lot more fun than that to live with now. My wife has her grumpy moments, but if you ask her she will say, "I don't always wake up grumpy. Sometimes I let him sleep." Seriously, my wife is fun to live with and she says I am getting to be that way. Keeping a positive attitude helps. I want to keep the attitude of the Army field commander who, when informed that he and his soldiers were completely surrounded, said: "Excellent! We can attack in any direction now!" My attitude makes a big difference towards being fun to live with.

Being fun to live with has always been associated with being joyful in my mind. *JOY!* What a fun word. A joy to be around! That is what I want to be. The *Scholastic Dictionary of Synonyms, Antonyms, Homonyms* lists the synonyms for joy: gladness, pleasure, delight, gaiety, merriment and hilarity, among others. If being around me meant the presence of these things, my goal would be accomplished.

Although I think they have more to do with happiness, that dictionary lists the antonyms of joy as sorrow, pain, trouble, misery. I'm sure you know people who you are sorry you have to be around, and some who are a pain to be around. These are people who revel in their trouble and misery and want their trouble and misery to be your trouble and misery. I don't want to be that kind of old man. Those people are not joyful, they are grumpy and I do not want to be a grumpy old man.

But, if I am, it may not be my fault. I look to science as my defense. Several years ago the *Journal of the International Neuropsychological Society* published an article titled "Humor comprehension in older adults." BBC News published a report on the article with the headline "Grumpy old people 'can't help it.'" It went on to say "Grumpy old men may not be able to help it, as age could affect their sense of humor, scientists have found." I could rest my case for grumpiness there, but if I did it would be resting on quicksand.

A little investigation into the details of the study that prompted the article in the *Journal of the International Neuropsychological Society* was revealing. It seems the researchers tested 40 people over 65 and 40 undergraduates in a university. Right there, you see, the deck is stacked against us old people. There are over 45 million of us old people in the US and they only tested 40. There are only 18 million undergraduates in the US, which means that there are almost three times as many old people as undergraduates and they tested 40, the same number as they did old people. The sample sizes were not proportionate to the population. But that's not all. The sample sizes were not nearly big enough. They should have tested more than 40 people out of groups that contain millions each.

Besides that, I don't think young people ought to be allowed to study and report findings on older people. The author of this study was born when I was graduating from high school. Younger people have not been where we are. How can they really know what we are like? Just because we don't think like they do doesn't mean they are right and we are wrong. I'll show you what I mean.

The participants in this study had to complete jokes and cartoon strips, choosing the "correct" punch line or final picture from a selection of options. The "correct" punch line is certainly a subjective point upon which to determine the humor of a joke. Here is one of the jokes on the test. "A businessman is riding the subway after a hard day at the office. A young man sits down next to him and says, 'Call me a doctor, call me a doctor'. The businessman asks, 'What's the matter, are you sick?'" The participants were expected to correctly identify the punch line as "The young man says, 'I just graduated from medical school'."

Now, when you have stopped laughing at that stupid joke, I will tell you that that joke has been around longer than the people doing the study and they got the "correct" punch line wrong. After the young man says, "Call me a doctor, call me a doctor," the businessman says, "OK, you're a doctor." Except it was an ambulance instead of a doctor. And the young man was not on a train, he was in the street having been hit by a car and the businessman said: "OK, you are an ambulance." That's why calling him an ambulance makes sense and why it is funny. Do you see what I mean? How can younger people say that, "age-related declines in short-term memory, abstract reasoning and moving between different thought trains may affect humor comprehension in old people" when they can't even get the joke right? No wonder they call us grumpy old people if they mess up a joke and we don't laugh.

I love science. Science is the only field of study where contradictions and conflicting theories abound and they have faith enough to believe today what they know could very well be disproved tomorrow. In other words, science never has a last word. And that is certainly true about what science says about old people. Unfortunately, many younger people form their opinion of old people based on scientific finds that are reported in the media. Fortunately, not all scientific finds find that old people lack cognitive ability and humor and are therefore grumpy.

More to my liking, a recent issue of *Psychology Today* published a column titled "The Myth of Age-Related Cognitive Decline." Need I say more? But I will, anyway. The column was a report on massive research done by five cognitive scientists and reported in the January, 2014, issue of The Wiley Online Journal *Topics in Cognitive Science*. These scientists came up with some findings that old people can sink their teeth in (and take them out if the Polident holds).

The report admits right off the bat that for a long time, behavioral scientists have thought that old age is associated with cognitive decline, and thus, with grumpiness. The findings of these scientists demonstrate that this way of thinking may be fundamentally wrong. Notice they say "may" be and not "is." They cannot say this is the way it is because science never has a last word. Sorry, I digress. Healthy aging, according to the report, "may be nothing more than gaining more experiences and then dealing with the consequences of having learned from that experience. To put it another way, you get slower when you're older because you're smarter." That's the smartest thing I have heard in a long time.

They further state, "as people get older, they gather more experiences, they learn more names for things, and they potentially better understand how the social and economic systems around them work." The result is that this makes them slower to respond because they have a larger database to consult before determining the best or correct response. Does that make sense, or what? When I buy a new computer, it does everything at lightning speed. But after five years of loading programs, saving documents, and searching the Internet the computer speed slows to a crawl because it has stored huge amounts of data that has to be consulted before a command is obeyed.

Or, for instance, think of a public library. If you want to find a copy of Charles Dickens' *Great Expectations* and there are only five other books in the library, you can find the one you want very quickly. However, if there are 50,000 other books in the library it would take considerably longer to find your *Great Expectations*. Now, if you are young you can run to the card catalog in the library computer, find the floor and shelf your *Expectations* are on and run out of the library faster than an older person could. But the point of the scientific research is to show that there just aren't 50,000 books in the library of a young person. And the point of my writing all this is to show that I do not have a scientific excuse for being a grumpy old man and, therefore, I am not going to use it. If I am grumpy it's because I want to be and I do NOT want to be a grumpy old man. I want to be an old man who keeps his wits about him and is fun to live with even though I might be cognitively slower.

What I really want to do in my old age is follow the example of Yogi Berra. Yogi was born in 1925, and that was not yesterday. He is a former Major League baseball player and manager with the New York Yankees, and was elected to the Baseball Hall of Fame in 1972. Yogi quit school after the eighth grade but that did not stop his learning, and when he retired from baseball he seemed to get real smart, becoming famous for using paradoxical contradictions in his speaking. Now how many of the younger generations do you know that can speak paradoxical contradictions? When he was in his late 70's, he made a television commercial with a duck for an insurance company. When settling a claim Yogi says, "And they give ya' cash, which is just as good as money!" What a fun old man! As he got older, Yogi was always careful because he did not want to make the wrong mistake. And neither do I. So you might be hearing more from Yogi later.

Now, back to this idea of me wanting to be an old man who is a joy to be around. I kind of got sidetracked. Joy has to come from a deep-down contentment with the kind of person you are and the circumstances God has put in your life. It is not an emotion of happiness that springs from a good happening in your life. Joy springs from what is inside you. As an old man I want to be a fountain of joy for those around me and especially for my wife. We lived in Scotland for five years and we learned the Scottish people have their own kind of joy. It is just not always the kind you think it is. I don't want to be like the thoughtful Scotsman who was heading out to the pub. As he was leaving he turned to his wee wifie and said, "Put your hat and coat on lassie." She replied, 'With joy, I'm glad you are taking me to the pub with you!' He replied, "It's not that. I'm just switching the central heating off while I'm out." That is not the kind of old man I want to be to live with.

When I was thinking about being a fun old man to be around, I started thinking about who could be a role model since I've never been an old man before. My mind immediately went to my Uncle Proctor. Uncle Proctor married my father's youngest sister and that is how he became my Uncle Proctor and how I learned that he was a person that was fun to be around. He was a fine Christian man and a perfect example that Christians can be fun and have fun.

I was four years old when he became my uncle and my family started visiting him and my aunt. They soon had two sons so as the years went on my brother and I had cousins to play with when we visited my aunt and Uncle Proctor. They lived on a farm and Uncle Proctor's farm was a fun farm (not a funny farm) to visit. He had a horse which he let us ride. He had an old Army jeep in which he let us ride. Later on as his sons got older, they had four-wheel dirt bikes that he let us ride. There was a fishing pond close to their house that we could fish in. There was always something fun to do at Uncle Proctor's and he was always fun to do them with.

After he quit farming, the farm did not cease to be a fun place and he did not cease to be fun to be around. He put in a nine-hole golf course and a big swimming pool and opened a golf and swim club so that his neighbors for miles around could come and have fun.

He was also fun for adults to be around, but I did not realize this until I became an adult. He met a lot of people he had never met before, but he never met a stranger. He could talk to anyone from garbage man to governor and after a few minutes you would think they grew up together. They would be laughing and swapping stories like old friends.

Speaking of stories, Uncle Proctor was always telling stories. When he got older he was always telling stories that he forgot he had already told us, but we didn't care. The fun was in his telling it. He had fun telling them and we had fun listening to him tell them. He was just a fun uncle to be around.

Uncle Proctor died in 2013. He is one man who left a hole in the water when God fished him out of the pond of life at age 82. That is the kind of old man I want to be, one that is fun to be around.

An element of being fun to live with involves being fun to be made fun of. One day I was going to lubricate the awning that covers the sliding glass door in our living room. This is necessary in southern Spain because of the sun and heat. So, I went to the cabinet and pulled out the can of spray lubricant. I went outside onto the terrace and Ann closed the door behind me so the spray would not go inside. I started to spray the awning and looked at the can. Then I showed the can to Ann through the sliding glass door. We both burst out laughing. I was going to lubricate the awning with shoe deodorizer. When I was younger, I would be careful to get the right can of spray from the cabinet. Now that I am older it didn't matter. It didn't matter because it became a laughing matter for us. It was more fun than if I had picked the right spray can.

To me, another element of being fun to live with is being spontaneous; being able to do something on the spur of the moment. During my years working as a Certified Public Accountant, almost every minute was scheduled with appointments and meetings written on a daily calendar. When God called us to be missionaries to Mexico, I found out that God does not have a watch or a calendar. I would plan to do something but something else more urgent would come up; then something else. After all that was done I would try to do what I had planned to do. During that first year as a missionary we never went to bed the same day we got up. I finally caught on and started making plans with the caveat, "*Si Dios quiere*" (if God wills or allows). Then we started taking things as they came, thus becoming spontaneous.

Spontaneity adds to the fun of life. My wife likes it when I spring a surprise on her by saying, "Let's go get an ice cream cone," or "Would you like to go out to breakfast instead of eating that rice cake?" The thing is, there is a time element involved in the phrase "spur of the moment." For me, change shoes and I am ready. For my wife, being spontaneous includes being patient. The other day we decided to do something spontaneous, so I changed shoes. Then I waited and waited and started making some comments that indicated I was tired of waiting and also was not fun to live with at the moment. My wife says to me, "You do not have any patience. I have been telling you for the last hour that I will be ready in five minutes!" What are you going to do but laugh?

For older people life tends to be routine, but it can still be fun to live—if you are fun to live with. My wife is fun to live with. The other day we were having coffee and she was talking. She paused, and I looked at her. Then she said, "I will continue this conversation when I remember what I was going to say." We laughed.

I read on that blessed internet (so it must be true) about a husband and wife who were stuck in traffic and their car engine stalled. The husband could not get it started and the car behind them started honking its horn—HONK, HONK, HONK! His wife got out and went back and said something to the driver of that car. The husband saw in the rearview mirror that the driver laughed. She came back and got in the car and then the husband saw the man who had been honking get out and come toward his window. "What did you say to him?" he asked. She said, "I just told him that if he would come up here and help you get the car started, I would stay back there and honk his horn for him." That could have been my wife.

You see, being fun to live with has to come from inside you. It comes from the kind of person you are and not necessarily what you do. That is the kind of old man I want to be.

[3]

Laconic

> "Old age is by nature rather talkative."
> —Marcus Tullius Cicero

CICERO WAS A ROMAN philosopher, politician, lawyer, orator, political theorist, consul and constitutionalist living in the first century BC. You might note that all those hats he wore necessitated the use of a lot of words. Besides being a speaker of many words he was also a prolific writer of many words. He only lived 63 years, but back then that was considered to be an old age. So he knew what he was talking about when he said old age was rather talkative.

I, on the other hand, want to be an old man who talks, but is not considered to be talkative. In other words, I want to be the kind of old man who talks in sentences and short paragraphs rather than one who talks in pages and chapters. I'm sure you know the kind of old people I am talking about. You make the standard greeting, "How are you?" and 30 minutes later you are looking for an excuse to get away.

The standard reply to the standard greeting of "How are you?" is "Fine, thank you." Maybe if there is a temporary problem one might say, "I have a headache, but I'm fine." Not some old people! If they happen to be fine today, yesterday their joints ached, but not like their cousin, "who has arthritis and who hasn't been able to walk without a cane since he was 40 years old. That's when he had the automobile accident that left him paralyzed from the waist down for 26½ years until he took some new wonder drug that made him start having some feeling in his toes, then his feet, then his legs, then his hips until finally he could walk again, but it left him with arthritis in every joint from the waist down. Now he walks with a cane but he thanks God he can walk. He also thanks his doctor, who is one of these foreign kind, from India or out East, or maybe he is Hawaiian, I'm not sure.

"These foreigners are taking over the medical system here but I guess it is because the young people in this country do not want to go to all the trouble to go to medical school so they can make the money a doctor makes. They want the money now and the banks will lend it to them with no collateral. Then they can't get a job making enough money to buy what they want plus pay off the credit-card debt so they don't pay the credit-card debt and the banks lose money and the government bails them out and then the government claims to not have enough money to pay full Social Security benefits. And it is all the young peoples' fault that don't want to work high paying jobs so they can pay into the Social Security system so there will be enough money in the system to pay my Social Security.

"My cousin was not like that before his accident. He had a good job paying in the maximum Social Security every year. The accident was his fault so he did not get any kind of millions of dollars settlement that the courts are giving now-a-days. Imagine, people getting paid in a lump sum a hundred times more than they could ever make in a lifetime of working just because of some accident. And they don't even have to pay Social Security taxes on that money, not that they would ever need to collect Social Security with all that money. But you never know. My next door neighbor collected $600,000 in a settlement from a company that made faulty false teeth; he kept biting his tongue with them. How long do you think he kept the money? He invested all of it in his son-in-law's Edsel dealership ... etc., etc., etc."

You know how it goes—on and on, and on and on. Well, I do not want to be that kind of talkative old man. In other words, I do not want the gift of speech without the gift of conversation. There is a proverb in the Bible that says, "When words are many, sin is not absent, but he who holds his tongue is wise." The ancient philosopher, Plato, must have read that proverb. He said, "Wise men speak because they have something to say; fools because they have to say something." I do not want to be the kind of old man who feels compelled to be talkative. In the book of Job in the Bible, Zophar the Naamathite asks Job, "Will your idle talk reduce men to silence?" I know of nothing more likely to reduce people to silence than the idle talk of an old man. After somebody has talked for two or three pages you don't want to say anything that may prompt them to talk several more pages. A quick exit is what you are looking for.

According to a National Institute of Mental Health survey done in July 2014, people's number one fear is the fear of public speaking. Now that does not hold true for many old people. Give them an audience of one or more and they can speak for an hour, no problem. And when they are finished it is not like it was some kind of catharsis, an emotional release which makes them feel better. They see it as a performance of which they are proud—proud that they remembered all those details.

God bless them, there are some people who do not mind listening to an old person for an hour. They have the patience for it. They even have the gift of seeming to be interested in hearing what is said. I hope that if I ever become a talkative old man, the Lord will put at least one person of this kind in my life.

Not boring

Old men who talk in pages and chapters tend to be boring and I do not want to be a boring old man. The French philosopher Voltaire said, "The secret to being a bore is to tell everything." He got that right. Telling everything takes chapters and chapters regardless of what "everything" is. Usually, somebody's "everything" includes some fiction along with the nonfiction. Yes, it seems like they are talking in books instead of paragraphs and chapters.

Someone once said, "Boredom is God's way of telling you that you are wasting time." Another spot-on comment on life. A boring talker is talking out of his own boredom and is speaking boredom to whoever he is talking to. Over the course of my life I have sat in many meetings listening to boring speakers, and I am sure you have too. What is going through your head as you sit there? Is it not, "What a waste of time!"? Of course, listening to a boring speaker is a waste of time. It is killing time and I do not want to be killing time (yours or mine) while time is killing me. I hope listening to me is never boring and a waste of time. That is not the kind of old man I want to be.

I do not want to be an old man who is talkative and boring. Therefore, I do not want to be the kind of old man who assumes people are more interested in hearing about my life than they are in telling me about theirs. It is not that I have not had what, for me, is an interesting life. I started out working as a

Certified Public Accountant for 25 years in the United States. How, you may ask, does that make for an interesting life? I did get to testify as an expert witness in a Federal securities fraud trial in which the party I testified for ended up in prison. But it wasn't my fault. And I did get involved in the accounting for a crooked state Senator who ended up in prison. But that wasn't my fault, either. And I did marry Ann, a woman who had been an aerobatic pilot and who had done air shows with the television hero Sky King. Of course, that was some years after the TV series ended. But you are not interested in all that.

The real experiences for us, which I am not going to tell you about, started when we became missionaries in 1993. God sent these two people who were used to the comforts of the business world (air conditioning, carpet, smooth roads, etc.) to a little village in the mountains of northern Mexico to live in an adobe house (for the younger generation, I am talking about the Spanish mud bricks, not the Internet application software company) with no running water. There we travelled one-lane roads built out of the side of mountains with no guard rails and if you looked over the side you could see wrecked vehicles a thousand feet down. The dealings we had with evil spirits or the supernatural experiences we had with border agents would not interest you at all.

I get tempted to tell people about our experiences in Sierra Leone, West Africa. The country was involved in a brutal civil war when we went there to work at a Bible college in a little village in the bush called Jui. But who wants to hear about that today? I have to be careful because if I get started I will tell about our first time in Freetown, the capital. We were staying in a smelly dump of a hotel (one of the few that were open) and there were a lot of men going in and out of the room across the hall from us, but they were always careful to have their door closed if we were around. One time we surprised them and their door was open. Inside we saw a bunch of men sitting in a circle surrounded by stacks of AK-47 assault rifles. Some rebels had infiltrated in to the capital and were hiding in our hotel. Thinking the hotel owner was part of them, we said nothing and kept a low profile until we could find another place to stay.

Now, if I was to go on with this story I would describe what it is like living in a war zone. We did not realize the Bible College was real close to rebel held territory. To get to Freetown we had to go through checkpoints where soldiers would stick the barrel of a machine gun in my face and ask for my papers. The rebels had government soldiers' uniforms, so the only way you could know if the checkpoint was legitimate was if they took stuff from your car. If they did, they were rebels. We had bombs going off near us and helicopter gunships shooting rockets into the hills about 2 miles from our campus. During all of this, the classes continued.

Gosh! You got me started now. If you have to go, just say so. Just living in the bush in Africa is an experience. But with brutal rebels around it was a thrill—to be avoided if at all possible. One weekend we did not realize that Ann and I were the only people on campus. Of course, the rebels chose that time to visit the campus. We saw them coming and we locked the doors and closed all the curtains to make the house look unoccupied. The rebels surrounded our home, tried the doors and, thinking there was nothing of value, they moved on. On previous visits to the campus, they had set fire to some buildings. We thank God they did not set fire to our house as that is what they usually did when they sacked a village.

Are you still listening? Or have I put you into a mental coma? Anyway, the rebels were not the only worry. Being in the bush we had a large number of snakes around our house. I came within two feet of stepping on a cobra one time and green mambas were constantly on our porch, and one even tried to come through our screen door with us sitting there watching it. The monkeys, bats, spiders, ants and termites we constantly dealt with paled in comparison. The many times we had malaria would bore you to death, if you are not already.

One more thing to illustrate God's providence. In 2001, the rebels had taken eleven British soldiers hostage and were keeping them in camps about 20 miles from us. There was a small airstrip behind our home. One morning, the strip filled with helicopters and a troop transport plane landed on the strip. Then some Chinook helicopters came. Soldiers left the plane and got in the helicopters. Then they all left. About an hour later they all came back and reversed the process, with the soldiers getting out of the helicopters and getting into the airplane. There seemed to be more soldiers this time. Then they all left and returned to a British aircraft carrier that was off of the coast. The British had staged a raid and rescued their soldiers. They lost one of their soldiers but killed over 200 rebels in the process. Some years later, we were living in Aberdeen, Scotland, working with drug addicts and alcoholics. One day I talked to a man who was on drugs. Turned out he had been in the British army in Sierra Leone and had participated in that raid to rescue their soldiers. The incident left him shell-shocked and he was discharged from the Army, suffering from Post Traumatic Stress Disorder, and had turned to drugs. I was able to tell him that we saw him on that fateful day.

O.K., one more one more thing and then I will let you go, if you are still there. Also in Aberdeen, I counseled a young man who had been in that raid in Sierra Leone and then been a sniper in the British army in Afghanistan. One day they sighted a target. He zeroed in and shot the target. When they went to check on the target, they also found the body of a small boy. The boy had been behind the target and the bullet killed both. This young man could not handle that, was discharged from the Army and ended up on drugs. He came to me because he wanted to confess to a religious person, doubting that God could ever forgive him for killing a child. I was able to remind him that he did not know the child was there, and if he had known, he would not have been allowed to shoot the target. He did not mean to kill the child and there was no sin involved in that. However, observing the way he was living, we were able to discuss other sins he was guilty of that needed to be confessed and repented of. That's what we do, you know.

Anyway, I have done what I said I did not want to do. I have talked pages and have become boring. Now you see what I mean and you see why I do not want to be the type of old man who does this.

Often people who talk a lot think that they know everything when the reality is that they were born stupid and greatly increased their birthright. I don't want to be the kind of old man who thinks he knows everything. I have found two things that are expanding that I cannot do anything about: knowledge and my waistline. My memory does not seem to want to expand with either one of these. I have forgotten at least one half of the things I ever knew. I have often heard it said that a picture is worth 1,000 words. Now I find out that a picture takes 3,000 times the memory as 1,000 words. Therefore, I have been selectively deleting pictures from my memory so that I can store more words. That should get me going in the right direction to eventually know everything I remember.

People who think they know everything will always give an answer. Voltaire said, "He must be very ignorant for he answers every question he is asked." He also said, "Judge a man by his questions rather than his answers." That is one way to keep from being a talkative old man—ask questions. That gives other people a chance to talk and indicates you value their opinion. And if you think their opinion is wrong, thank them for sharing it, don't start an argument. Again Voltaire: "Opinion has caused more trouble on this little earth than plagues and earthquakes." Talkative old men can be troublesome old men and that is not the kind of old man I want to be. You see, I want people to want to be around me. Therefore, I do not want to be talkative, troublesome or boring. C.S. Lewis said, "It is much easier to pray for a bore than to go see one." I want to be the kind of old man who people want to go see.

Operations and illnesses

Nothing gets old people talking like rehearsing operations and illnesses. You know the kind of old person I mean, you ask them how they are doing and they give you an organ recital. I do not want to be the kind of old man who constantly talks about his operations and illnesses (even though I have had some). Some old people are even proud of their list of health issues and delight in talking about them to anyone who will listen.

It really doesn't matter to me if people know that my wife almost died of typhus in Mexico, or that I had to be medevaced out of Sierra Leone because I had aplastic anemia, tuberculosis, malaria and another bacteria in my lungs (that when I got back to the States even the Center for Disease Control could not identify), all at the same time, spending a year in a wheelchair and taking two years to get well. Or that I had sinus surgery in Aberdeen and the surgeon accidently penetrated the lining of my brain allowing infection in that caused me to have Bacterial Meningitis. But I will be glad to tell someone if they are interested. Otherwise, I do not want to be the kind of old man who goes on and on about their operations and illnesses.

Does not exaggerate

I have noticed that when old people get to talking, whether it is about their families, their accomplishments or their operations and illnesses, they tend to exaggerate. American humorist Josh Billings said, "There are some people so addicted to exaggeration that they can't tell the truth without lying." Now, it is certainly not the intent of an old person to lie when talking about their families, accomplishments and operations and illnesses. Sometimes the memory expands as they (we) remember things. Or, sometimes, we remember things to be the way we want them to be rather than the way they really are. There is no intent to lie, it just comes out. That is a problem with us missionaries who have to give reports back home to sending churches. The temptation is to speak "evangelastically" when telling the number of conversions. Does exaggeration or stretching the truth make it a lie? Or is it just an oversized truth?

Lebanese poet Khalil Gibran had this to say: "Exaggeration is truth that has lost its temper." Puns are one of my favorite forms of humor, but I am not sure Gibran was being punny when he said what he said about exaggeration. Exaggeration may be truth that has gone mad, but I think he probably had the archaic definition of temper in mind: a middle state between extremes. He was born in the nineteenth century and that is the way he would have talked.

On a side note, did you know that Khalil Gibran is the third best-selling poet of all time, behind Shakespeare and Laozi. Who is Laozi?, you may ask. He was a philosopher and poet who lived in China in the fourth-century BC. He wrote the *Tao Te Ching* and was the founder of Taoism. Of course the Bible is the best-selling book of all time and it contains poetry. But nobody buys it for the poets themselves. Anyway, this is the kind of information old men tend to interject into conversations that really turns people off. It turns a conversation into a monologue and I do not want to be the kind of old man who does that.

I'm sorry! Back to exaggeration. I'm sure you have heard old people talking about their families and you know the truth is stretched. My brother and sister-in-law own a lot of acreage with a lake on it. Well, actually it is a small fishing pond, if you see what I mean. When some old people start talking about their families you just know their family tree, unlike mine, is kind of shady. If you know anything about their families at all, you know their gene pool needs some more chlorine in it. They exaggerate their family's character and accomplishments. My main concern as an old man is that my family does not have to exaggerate to speak highly of me. And, I am sorry to say, I should have started 40 years ago.

Giving advice

Old people, especially old men, like to give advice to the younger generations. That really adds to the frustration of being an old man because, more and more, the younger generations do not want advice from old people. Therefore, to keep my frustration level down I do not want to be the kind of old man who insists on giving advice. The late television commentator, Andy Rooney, shared what he had learned, "...that it is best to give advice in only two circumstances: when it is requested and when it is a life-threatening situation."

That sounds like good advice to me. To give unsolicited advice puts people in a quandary. What do they do with it? Do they ignore it? Agatha Christie said, "Good advice is always certain to be ignored, but that is no reason not to give it." That really does sound like an old person talking. Ignoring good advice might work for some. Usually they are radicals of some kind. That jack-of-all-trades G.K. Chesterton claims, "I owe my success to having listened respectfully to the very best advice, and then going away and doing the exact opposite." Among other things, Chesterton was a lay theologian but he didn't believe the Bible where it says in Proverbs 12:15: "The way of a fool seems right to him, but a wise man listens to advice." On the other hand, you have a famous comedian saying, "A word to the wise ain't necessary, it's the stupid ones who need advice." So what does an old man do?

Old men think they are qualified, and sometimes overly qualified, to give advice. We have a long history of life experiences and have learned a lot by having observed a lot. According to Yogi Berra you can observe a lot just by watching, and I have watched a lot of changes take place in society, most of which I observe to be dehumanizing, but that is the subject for another book.

I, personally, try to restrain from giving unsolicited advice even though I should be qualified to give it. I have three postgraduate degrees, two of them doctorates and I have learned a lot by making a lot of mistakes. Most of these were made when I was in my 20's and 30's and not open to receiving advice from old people. Like Yogi, if I could help young people from making wrong mistakes I would like to do it.

As an old man, I want to talk about my experiences, my illnesses, and to give advice. But as an old man who wants to be liked, I need to hold my tongue and keep my advice to myself. I may as well. The author John Steinbeck said, "You know how advice is. You only want it if it agrees with what you wanted to do anyway." It is useless to give that kind of advice. So, I'm going to save my breath, since I probably don't have much left. Germain G. Glien said, "The older I grow the more I listen to people who don't talk much." That is the kind of old man I want to be.

Listening instead of talking

I am going to end this chapter on being a talkative old man by talking a little about listening. Listening is a lost art in our society today. "You are not listening to me!" is the cry of parents to children and children to parents. It seems like everybody wants to talk and nobody wants to listen. My wife says I never listen to her. At least I think that is what she said (just kidding!). Politicians do not listen to their constituency except at election time. They have to listen then so they can repeat back what they hear in the form of promises that are forgotten after the election.

In my older years I see two things attached to listening that I did not see some years ago. Those two things are caring and learning.

I believe there is a dearth of listening because there is a dearth of caring. People don't care what other people say because they only care about themselves and do not care about the one talking. Or at least that is the impression given. Just today, my wife said something to me and I did not respond. She immediately thought I did not care. I never want to give her that impression, because it is not true. Therefore, I need to be the kind of old man who listens and responds. Talking, listening, responding makes communication. Communication makes relationships. Relationships, even more than memories, are the treasures of old age.

Listening and learning go hand in hand. Jared Sparks said, "When you talk, you repeat what you already know; when you listen, you often learn something." He ought to know, for he was president of Harvard College and a minister of the Gospel in the 1800's. Those two professions depend on people listening to learn. Novelist Ernest Hemingway said, "I like to listen. I have learned a great deal from listening carefully. Most people never listen." That's because they never stop talking. According to writer Ken Fracaro, "We listen in order to learn and retain information. If we are speaking, we are not listening or learning anything to add to our sum of knowledge. That is why the first step to effective listening is to stop talking!"

I am writing this in the chapter on being a talkative old man because I don't want to be one, and the way to not be one is to stop talking and to start listening. At my age I am more concerned with listening in the context of personal one-on-one conversations when I am having conversations with friends or potential friends. There are people who need to know you care about them and the way they will know is if you show interest in their lives by listening to learn what is important to them and what is going on in their lives. I said in Chapter 1 that I want to be a loveable old man and that means that, to me, I should see other people as more important than I am. What better way is there to make other people feel important and that you care about them than really listening to them to learn what makes them tick. The philosopher Epictetus pointed out, "We have two ears and one mouth so that we can listen twice as much as we speak."

In concluding this chapter, I remind myself that I do not want to be the kind of old man who is talkative; that is, I want to be an old man who talks in sentences and short paragraphs, rather than in pages and chapters. Here are some Proverbs from the Bible that I need to keep in mind:

Let the wise listen and add to their learning and let the discerning get guidance (1:5).

A man of knowledge uses words with restraint, and a man of understanding is even-tempered (17:27).

Even a fool is thought wise if he keeps silent, and discerning if he holds his tongue (17:28).

He who answers before listening—that is his folly and his shame (18:13).

Old people need to understand the economics of their situation: talk is cheap because supply exceeds demand.

[4]

Carpe diem

"Yesterday is gone. Tomorrow has not yet come.
We have only today. Let us begin."
— Mother Teresa

  CARPE DIEM IS A LATIN APHORISM usually translated as "seize the day," taken from a poem in the *Odes* (book 1, number 11) written in 23 BC by the poet Horace. *Carpe* is the second-person singular present active imperative of *carpō* "pick or pluck" used to mean "enjoy, seize, use, make use of." *Diem* is the accusative case of the noun *dies* "day." A more literal translation of *carpe diem* would thus be "enjoy the day" or "pluck the day [as it is ripe]"—i.e., to enjoy the moment.

  In Horace, the phrase is part of the longer "*carpe diem, quam minimum credula postero*," which can be translated as "Seize the day, put very little trust in tomorrow (the future)." The ode says that the future is unforeseen and that one should not leave to chance future happenings, but rather one should do all one can today to make one's future better. The phrase *carpe diem* is often used differently in contemporary popular culture, to justify reckless behavior (YOLO, you only live once). The meaning of *carpe diem* as used by Horace is not to ignore the future, but rather not to trust that everything is going to fall into place for you and taking action for the future today.

I want to be the kind of old man who seizes the day. My use of the term is more in line with the Urban Dictionary meaning of seizing "a certain moment in time; to make the most out of that part of time." In other words, I want to make the most of "today" because I realize that my "todays" are numbered and I want to take advantage of every opportunity to be the kind of old man I say I want to be.

Virginia Ironsides wrote, "I can't help feeling we are the luckiest generation alive. Just as we are starting to lose our memories, what happens?—Along comes Wikipedia." That takes care of the memory problem of being an old man. To take care of the mobility problem, driverless cars are coming. For me, part of *carpe diem* means to seize the tools available to help you accomplish what you want to accomplish today. That is why I copied the first two paragraphs of this chapter from the Wikipedia webpage on *carpe diem*. It is there, it is free, it is not copyrighted, why not seize it?

Lives in the present, not the past

Old people are said to be "living in the past" when they talk about things that happened in their past. But for them (us) the past is much longer than the prospective future. The past contains events that have actually happened. The future for an old person is "iffy" at best. That is why you hear them (us) joking about not buying green bananas. The future will certainly not be as long as the past and there are no certain events in the future. But, as Mother Teresa said, the past is gone and the future has not come (and may not come). What we have is today, this moment, and we need to seize it remembering that it is a gift from God and there is good to be done.

The good to be done today could be as simple and easy as a kind word. Andy Rooney died in his 90's, but before he died he left us a list of some things that he had learned in those 90+ years. He said, "I have learned that just one person saying to me 'You've made my day!' makes my day." How easy it is to make someone's day that way. That's how to *carpe diem*.

Stays current

I want to be the kind of old man who lives in the present and not in the past. Someone asked Yogi Berra what time it was and he responded, "You mean now?" He wanted to stay real current. The nineteenth-century Baptist preacher Charles Spurgeon said, "A cake made of memories will do for a bite now and then, but it makes poor daily bread." What happened in the past may have been the cause of what is happening now, but it will not sustain the present. The present needs today's daily bread, today's opportunities, and today's current conditions and events in order for it to be called "today."

If I am going to stay current in my old age, I need to make a conscious effort to do so. I still haven't learned how to listen to both sides of a CD. (I assume you can as we just bought a DVD that was recorded on both sides. I wondered why it did not have a label on it. Now we are current on DVDs, as of today.) The older I get the easier it is to let things slide, to let the world pass on by while I enjoy what I did yesterday. That will not work for someone who wants to *carpe diem*. If you haven't noticed, things in this world are changing at break-neck speed, hourly rather than daily. So much of the world is driven by technology and technology is driven by money. Once most households had a television it stopped the flow of money to the television manufacturers. Therefore, a need for new televisions was created. Well, you know how it goes. People's lust for the latest means new communication devices almost daily. If I am going to stay current, I need to be able to communicate on the latest gadgets, otherwise, how will people know I am hip? (Not the joint that is on each side of the body below the waist that may eventually need replacing; but aware of or following the latest trends.)

One might think that watching television would be the way to stay current today and one may be right. You see the current events, current fashion, and current sociological trends, and you hear the current lingo. Or at least you are exposed to some producer's or some network's perspective on these things. It is a very popular communications medium. However, I do not watch television.

There are a number of reasons I do not watch television, but the main reason I do not watch television is what is on the television to watch. When we lived in Scotland, there was an annual television license fee to pay. That was for the privilege of watching BBC. You would think that having to pay a license fee for television, the programming would not have advertising, but that was not the case. There you have to have a license to watch advertising. Anyway, I digress. We did not have a television so I sent in the form saying we did not have a television. Some weeks later a British TV detective showed up at our door to inspect our home to make sure we did not have a television. As he was coming in, I told him that we valued our minds so we didn't watch television. He agreed and turned around and left.

When it comes to television, I agree with Groucho, Marx who said, "I find television very educating. Every time somebody turns on the set, I go into the other room and read a book."

My wife and I are readers, not watchers. We do not have to watch television because we see the effects of it on the streets. There is a lot of profanity, sex, and violence on TV and we see the same in real life. Too bad that in this fallen world it cannot work the other way. There is a lot of comedy on television, but so very little of it in real life (that is why I want to be an old man who is fun to live with). Seems like only the bad behavior gets learned from TV and repeated in real life. Someone said, "98 percent of American homes have TV sets, which means the other two percent of the households have to generate their own sex and violence." There is so much sarcasm in television programming today that that has become the way people talk to each other. Sarcasm has become the humor of choice on TV, and it is not funny. And television programming is dumb. When we had a television, I noticed it had a brightness control but it did not work. I turned it up all the way but the programs got dumber.

I know I am going on and on about this (already on the second page), but it is a pet peeve of mine. I want to stay current and I want to communicate with people. But with many people, if you cannot talk about what was on TV last night they have nothing to say. I hate to see what TV is doing to people. I talked to one person who said she liked the Home Shopping Network because it was commercial-free. I heard another one say that most of the guests on daytime talk shows are female, but of course they were not born that way.

I am not alone in my disdain for television. I'll share this and then move on so as not to bore you any longer because I do not want to be a boring old man. To show that I am current on something and that I can use recent inventions, I give you these quotes gleaned from the Internet:

"Television is a medium because anything well done is rare."
—Fred Allen

"What do you get when you add media to democracy? You get mediocracy."
—Peter Bergman

"When I got my first television set I stopped caring so much about close relationships."
—Andy Warhol

"Watching cable news because you want to be informed is like going to Olive Garden because you want to live in Italy."
—Andy Borowitz

"One of the few good things about modern times: If you die horribly on television, you will not have died in vain, you will have entertained us."
—Kurt Vonnegurt

"We can put television in its proper light by supposing that Gutenberg's great invention had been directed at printing only comic books."
—Robert M. Hutchins

In my efforts to *carpe diem* I will have to *carpe* something besides television. End of venting!

At the time I am writing this, the latest thing is "social media." Social media is the social interaction among people in which they create, share or exchange information, ideas, and pictures/videos in virtual communities and networks. Virtual communities exist only on the Internet. Am I with it so far? Today (the particular day I am writing this) some of the most popular social media websites are Facebook, Twitter, Linkedin, Pinterest, Instagram, Flicks, My Space, and many more. There is no telling what they will be when you read this. The point is, if we as old people want to stay current, we need to learn how to use social media. We need to do that if we want to communicate with any of the younger generations.

Me, I am stuck at e-mail and telephone calls. Therefore, I don't hear from many people. If I want to hear about my young friend's vacation, I have to go to his Facebook page. I can't call him because he keeps his phone turned off so he can Twitter and text without interruption. If he does answer or e-mail, it is in Twitter format. There is no "Dear Jack" or "Love you both." It is not even complete sentences or complete words, just abbreviations without interpretations. The older I get, the more I value the human presence of family and friends; the more I value the face-to-face communication of presence. Social media does not communicate presence to me and quite often it does not communicate true feelings. I guess I am failing at staying current. Maybe I will *carpe mañana*.

Content

As I write this we are living in Spain. One Spanish word can have several different meanings based on the context. The word "content" is a word like that in English. Of course, the content of this book is what I am writing here. But I am not talking about content; I am talking about content. Content meaning being satisfied with things as they are. One cannot *carpe diem* and enjoy today if one is not content.

The Apostle Paul wrote in the Bible:

> *I know what it is to be in need, and I know what it is to have plenty. I have learned the secret of being content in any and every situation, whether well fed or hungry, whether living in plenty or want. I can do everything through him who gives me strength"* (Philippians 4:12–13).

Now, this man is not just saying that off the top of his head. If you know his story, you know he wrote that from prison. Before that he had been shipwrecked, stoned, beaten with rods and living with his very life in danger. And yet, he was content. Proverbs 19:23 in the Bible says: "The fear of the Lord leads to life: Then one rests content, untouched by trouble." That is the kind of Christian I want to be and the kind of old man I want to be.

If I am going to *carpe diem*, I must be *suo contentum esse*. You will not learn what that means by watching television! But, on the other hand, you may be content to not know what it means. That is the kind of contentment I am talking about.

If God has blessed you with a spouse, that is where your contentment needs to begin. I am very content with my wife. She is a good wife. She doesn't complain about the little money I spend. And when I remind her that money doesn't grow on trees, she reminds me that, if that is so, why do banks have branches? You gotta love her! I am content at home and the home is a good place to learn to be content.

I learned a lot about being content from this dog we used to have. She was a female dog and she was the picture of contentment. This dog was content to use instincts instead of asking for directions. She was content to limit her time in the bathroom to a quick drink. She was very content when my friends came over. She was content with her body. She was content for me to come home late, in fact, the later I came home the happier she was to see me. She was content to not know about every other dog we've had. She was content to not receive presents on birthdays and Christmas. She was content not to criticize. You get the point. If ~~my wife~~ I could be as content as that dog was...

I need to be content in the present because I can't predict what the future holds. Yogi Berra says, "It's tough to make predictions, especially about the future." So, I need to be content now. And I need to be content with what I have and with not having everything I think I want. Epictetus expressed the key to contentment when he said, "He is a wise man who does not grieve for the things which he has not, but rejoices for those which he has." Another thing Andy Rooney learned is, "that we should be glad God doesn't give us everything we ask for." Yes, I am content with what God has provided and what he has withheld. I will *carpe contentus* and rejoice in the fact that the older I get the less peer pressure I have to make me discontent.

Grateful

I want to be the kind of old man who lives each day with an attitude of gratitude. The philosopher Cicero said, "Gratitude is not only the greatest of virtues, but the parent of all the others." Being grateful forces you to acknowledge a source of good outside of yourself. As a Christian I find the highest source of good in God. Psalm 106:1 tells me, "Give thanks to the Lord, for he is good. His love endures forever." I am grateful that I not only know God's love for me, but I know that there are some people who know me, and in spite of that, love me.

Gratitude is something I find in short supply in the world today. I was taught as a child to say "Please" when I asked for something and "Thank you" when (if) I received it. That taught me what was then polite manners, but it did not teach me to be grateful. Most of the time I was asking for what I knew I was going to get anyway. That does not foster an attitude of gratitude but an attitude of entitlement.

When I say I find gratitude in short supply in the world today, I am talking about a generation of youth and young adults who come along when governments are big and socialistic and credit is given if you can provide an address. This generation is not working for things and is naive enough to believe they are working to pay for things they already bought on credit. They have been given the things that my generation and my father's generation had to work for. My parents saved up for our first television set. They saved up to buy a newer used car. If you reach adulthood thinking you are entitled to these things, it is hard to be grateful when they come.

Now, you might think I am just a complaining old man and I begrudge the fact that this generation has things they don't need without working for them. I only begrudge the fact that gratitude has gone out the window. Maybe an example will show you what I am talking about. Twenty years ago when you went into a retail store, clerks were around and were pleased to help you find what you were looking for. Now in most retail stores, you have to hunt for someone to help you and most likely they will be doing something on their new Smartphone and will not like to be interrupted. Twenty years ago when you paid for something in that retail store, the cashier would say something like, "Thank you for shopping with us." I don't know about where you live, but here in Spain, the people paying for something are the ones saying, "Thank you" as if they are grateful that somebody took their money. The cashiers say, "See you later."

I guess I do sound like a grumbling old man, but I can tell you that the lack of gratitude in people is not something I am grateful for. I want to be an old person who is grateful. Yogi Berra was such a grateful old person and he knew how to return a compliment. When a woman told him he looked real cool, he replied, "Thanks, you don't look so hot yourself." Maybe that is not what I am talking about.

Maybe this story will illustrate what I am talking about. There was a godly farmer who was invited to lunch in the home of a city gentleman who was well-known for his modern and enlightened attitude that did not include gratitude. Before they ate the farmer bowed his head and said a prayer of thanks to God for the food on the table. When he finished, his host said, "You are wasting your breath giving thanks to God for this food, I provided it. That is an old-fashioned idea you have there." The farmer answered that it was his custom to pray and thank the Lord for his food, but "there are some on my farm who never pray a prayer of thanksgiving over their food." His host replied, "Well, there you are. There are some enlightened people on your farm. Are they your enlightened children?" "No, they are my pigs," the farmer answered.

Or maybe this story about Rudyard Kipling will better illustrate what I am talking about. He was an English writer living at the turn of the twentieth century. At one time he was so popular that he was being paid ten shillings per word, which was a lot of money back then. There was a group of college students that did not appreciate his writings. They sent him a facetious letter enclosing ten shillings and asked him to send them his best word. They got back a letter from Kipling that said, "Thanks." In the midst of facetiousness, he found a reason to be grateful.

In Chapter 1, I said that I was writing this with the very likely possibility of a nursing home being in my future. No doubt, if I live long enough I will need someone to take care of me. When that time comes, I definitely want to be an old man with an attitude of gratitude. Motivational blogger Ralph Marston gives this advice: "Make it a habit to tell people thank you. To express your appreciation sincerely and without the expectation of anything in return. Truly appreciate those around you, and you'll soon find many others around you. Truly appreciate life, and you'll find that you have more of it." Now, that to me is good nursing home advice. Another thing that Andy Rooney learned is that under everyone's hard shell is someone who wants to be appreciated and loved. That someone could be my caregiver.

Expressing gratitude to those who care for you, even though they are getting paid to do it, is a way to increase their pay. If you have ever worked, you know that getting paid to do a job and then receiving heartfelt gratitude for the job you do is like getting paid more than you agree to. In other words, gratitude adds value to services rendered. It particularly adds value to the people rendering the service. Whether it's my wife or strangers in a nursing home, I want to add value to them. By feeling gratitude towards them, I make them become more valuable to me. By expressing gratitude to them, I become more valuable to them and they feel more value in their care. Gratitude must be expressed. Someone said that feeling gratitude and not expressing it is like wrapping a present and not giving it. Sounds right to me.

Spain is different from anywhere else we have lived. The Spaniards like to exercise their right to *hacer manifestaciónes*. These are public demonstrations that could be political party supporters, football supporters, students who failed exams, people whose dwellings have been foreclosed on, or a club that wants to have a little parade. We like to learn the culture and know what is going, on so when one of these *manifestaciónes* is happening we usually check it out. Well, we just had one that sounded different. Since I am busy writing this, my wife went down to the street to see it. She just came in and said that it was worth seeing but was not worth going to see. What could I say but "Thank you"?

In 1 Thessalonians 5, the Bible tells me, "Be joyful always; pray continually; give thanks in all circumstances, for this is God's will for you in Christ Jesus." If it is God's will for me to give thanks in all circumstances then I want to do it, even if I do not have all I want. I can be thankful that I do not have everything I desire because if I did I would have nothing to look forward to. French novelist Alphonse Karr wrote, "Some people grumble that roses have thorns; I am grateful that thorns have roses." There is a lot I could learn from that.

I leave this section on being grateful with this thought. The next time you are in a group of people who are sharing things they are grateful for, say this, "I'm grateful that I did not get caught," and say no more.

No bitterness

If I am going to be the kind of old man who lives each day to the full, I cannot afford to have bitterness in my heart. Bitterness is a day killer that kills in more ways than one. Another thing that Andy Rooney learned was, "that when you harbor bitterness, happiness will dock elsewhere." Now that is a true truth for you. There are reasons that harboring bitterness causes happiness to dock elsewhere. One is that oil and water do not mix, and another is that two different things cannot occupy the same space at the same time.

But first, let's define what bitterness is. There appears to be as many different definitions as there are psychologists and dictionaries. One definition describes bitterness as that hateful, spiteful and resentful sourness in the heart that creeps in when you have been, or think you have been, maliciously wronged. Another says bitterness is a frozen form of latent anger and resentment. Another says it is holding on to or showing feelings of intense animosity, resentment or vindictiveness. The most common word association in the definitions is bitterness and resentment.

Resentment is the feeling of a negative emotion, such as anger or hatred, felt as a result of a real or perceived wrong done against you. Etymologically, the word originates from the French *ressentir*, with *re* being a prefix meaning "again" attached to the verb *sentir* meaning "to feel." When a perceived wrong is remembered, the feelings of anger or hatred attached to the wrong are felt again. They are felt again, over and over, each time the precipitating event is remembered, which is almost constantly. Dwelling on the wrong keeps the attached feelings in a heightened state which eventually results in bitterness in the seat of the emotions. It takes control and becomes the dominant emotion the affected person feels. The steady stream of resentment flowing into the pool of emotions poisons it and makes it bitter. Some say it is like drinking rat poison hoping the rat dies. That says it good.

Now, there are certain consequences to bitterness and that is the main reason that I do not want to be a bitter old man, today or any day. I've done the research (you can do it yourself if you don't accept my findings) and harboring bitterness brings consequences that affect you physically, mentally, emotionally, and spiritually. Physically, it causes chemical imbalances in various glands, weakens the immune system, causes fatigue and makes a person look like death warmed over. Mentally and emotionally, it leads to depression and stress. Spiritually, it brings doubts about one's relationship with God and could even make one question the existence of God. For example, that noted German philosopher Friedrich Nietzsche stated that "Nothing consumes a man more quickly than the emotion of resentment [bitterness]." The thing he is most noted for was his proclamation that "God is dead!" Nietzsche's father was a Lutheran pastor who brought him up in the Christian faith. But later on Nietzche fell into the bitterness trap and had a mental breakdown. He died a bitter old man. I do not want to live or die a bitter old man.

In one of Leo Tolstoy's shorter works titled *Family Happiness*, the main protagonists have just had a marital spat. After a terse comment by the husband, Sergey, the wife, Masha, has this thought: "It was the first time I had heard from him such bitterly sneering words. And the sneer did not put me to shame, but offended me; and the bitterness did not alarm me, but infected me." That is what bitterness does. It infects everyone that comes in contact with it. It has been said that holding on to the wrong that caused hurt and bitterness is like grabbing a rattlesnake by the tail. You are going to be bitten and the poison of bitterness will permeate your total being until death occurs. Such a death is more far-reaching than your own being because it can potentially destroy those around you as well. There is an antidote for this poison that I will talk about a little later.

Before that, there is something going on in mental health science about bitterness that may interest you. The book of Job in the Bible was written over 3,000 years ago. In Chapter

25, Job says, "Another man dies in bitterness of soul, never having enjoyed anything good." Also in the Bible, the book of Hebrews Chapter 12 says, "See to it that no one misses the grace of God, that no bitter root grows up to cause trouble and defile many." Roots grow under the ground where you can't see them. But they are alive and sprout the same thing above ground that is in the root. It has taken psychology and psychiatry thousands of years to realize the truth of what the Bible says about bitterness, resulting now in it being a diagnosed mental disorder.

Pathological reactions to adverse life events are heavily studied by mental health professionals. They continually expand clinical diagnostic classifications, thereby having more disorders to treat. You have heard of "Post-Traumatic Stress Disorder" (PTSD). Now that classification has been expanded to include a sub group called "Post-Traumatic Embitterment Disorder" (PTED). Yes, being a bitter person has become a recognized mental illness. No doubt it does cause pathological problems, but the cure is not therapy or pills. The cure is coming.

First, I am going to do something that I said in Chapter 3 that I did not want to do. But it is OK because I know I am doing it. I am going to talk for a page or two about something that is going on in the mental health sciences that really miffs me. From time to time the American Psychiatric Association (APA) publishes the *Diagnostic and Statistical Manual of Mental Disorders* (DSM). The first one (DSM-I) was published in 1952 and the most recent one (DSM-V) was published in 2013. It gives the standard criteria for the diagnosis and classification of mental disorders. The DSM is the "bible" of the mental health industry (I use the word "industry" instead of "profession" on purpose). It is relied on as sustainable evidence by practitioners, researchers, health insurance companies, pharmaceutical companies, the Federal Drug Administration, and the legal system. If that book says you are sick, everybody must recognize that you are sick.

Now, here's the rub. DSM-I published in 1952 listed 106 mental disorders. DSM-V lists 297 mental disorders, and because they did not want to keep increasing the number of disorders they have many more disorders as "subtypes" of listed disorders. They are broadening the net to catch more people. But there are consequences.

For instance, consider the above-mentioned Post-Traumatic Embitterment Disorder, which was added as a subtype of adjustment disorder. Harboring a grudge or resentment and anger is something that human beings tend to do until they figure out that it doesn't do any good. Now it is a recognized mental disorder. What are the knock-on effects of this? Remember, the precipitating event to the embitterment can be real or imagined. If caused by a person, it could be intentional or unintentional. By giving embitterment a recognized diagnosis, it gives it a different life. It authenticates the person or event that caused the resentment leading to bitterness and it justifies feelings of resentment and bitterness by the "victim." The embittered person can point to the diagnosis and then point to the person who is the perceived cause and say, "See there, you made me sick!" Of course, a few people do need professional help, but this is a danger I see in the present trend of mental disorder diagnosis.

DSM-V broadens the mental disorder net by including 15 new mental illness classifications. Many of them deal with ordinary humps in the road of life, stressful situations that almost all people encounter. Here is a sample of new disorders:

Cannabis Withdrawal (CNW) – If you want to quit smoking pot, you might have a mental disorder.

Hoarding Disorder (HD) – Can you close your closet door?

Hypersexual Disorder (HSD) – The way it is defined, every teenage boy has it.

Premenstrual Dysphoric Disorder (PMDD) – Looks like if a woman uses her monthly period as an excuse not to do something she has it.

Caffeine Withdrawal (CFW) – If you are grumpy in the morning before you have had your cup of coffee, you have it. The only way not to get it is don't quit.

Binge Eating Disorder (BED) – After living some years in the bush in Africa we were back in the US and went to Krispy Kreme and bought a dozen hot donuts and sat in the parking lot and ate all of them, but that is not this.

Rapid Eye Movement Sleep Behavior Disorder (REMSBD) – This is life imitating art based on the Hollywood movie *Sleepwalk With Me*. No kidding!

Restless Legs Syndrome (RLS) – If you get your kicks while you are asleep, you got it.

Avoidant/Restrictive Food Intake Disorder (ARFID) – Are you a picky eater? Avoid Brussels sprouts? Symptoms typically show up in childhood. Really?

Disinhibited Social Engagement Disorder (DSED) – This is directed at children who are inattentive and impulsive, as all children are.

Dysruptive Mood Dysregulation Disorder (DMDD) – This is limited to children under 18 who have what we used to call temper tantrums, surely a rare occurrence.

These last three just prove what my parents said all along—childhood is a mental disorder that they hoped I would grow out of. Not so! I have never been tested, but my wife says I have sleep apnea. And the disorder net has been expanded to catch me, as there is another new mental disorder classification called Central Sleep Apnea and Sleep-Related Hypoventilation (CSASRH). As with many of these classifications, your psychiatrists will fight with your medical doctor over who gets to treat you.

If you have heard enough of this, you can excuse yourself, step away from the book and come back in a couple of pages. This broadening of mental disorder classifications just miffs me. It seems like society keeps throwing things at you that prompts mental disorders. Technology changes so rapidly that it makes my head spin and my brain hurt—which is probably some kind of disorder. Anyway, take the Internet for example. I found this TechHive website that pointed out some new mental disorders caused by the Internet. These are not just reclassifications of old syndromes. They did not exist before Bill Clinton was President of the United States (although he may not be the cause). Do you have:

Facebook depression (FD) – Depression caused by negative posts about you or lack of social interaction on your Facebook page.

Phantom Ringing Syndrome (PRS) – When your brain makes you think your phone is vibrating in your pocket.

Nomophobia (NMP) – The anxiety caused by not having access to the Internet on your mobile device (No Mobile).

Internet Addiction Disorder (IAD) – A constant and unhealthy urge to access the Internet.

Online Gaming Addiction (OGA) – Self-explanatory.

Cyberchondria (CC) – The tendency to believe you have the diseases you read about online in the worst case scenario. For instance, this was posted on one website dealing with the new DSM-V disorders, "I just found out about ARFID today and cannot even begin to describe the relief I feel in knowing that I am not alone ... I have always been a 'picky eater'." Now this person is sick!

The Google Effect (TGE) – The tendency of the human mind to retain less information because it knows that all the answers are only a few clicks away.

This is one that they missed. I call it:

Psyco-pedia (PP) – The delusion that people who post and edit articles on Wikipedia are smarter than you are. They are subject to The Google Effect just like you are and they search, copy and paste just like you do.

See what I mean? We humans keep inventing ways to make ourselves sick. And if we don't do it, the APA will do it for us.

Oh, me! I need to go back and read Chapter 3 again. I am becoming quite talkative and jumping from here to there with my subjects. You might have noticed how the mental health profession has a propensity to use initials for disorders. This use of initials for longer names of things and phrases has become another disorder in society, in my opinion. It is endemic in social network communications. For example, one you see a lot is LOL. Now that can mean Lots of Love, a positive connotation, or Lots of Luck, a negative connotation. The more common meaning is Laugh Out Loud, which can be positive or negative according to its context. It is endemic in academia in all fields from sciences to theology. For example, a journal published by a philosophical society I belong to contains these sentences I picked at random:

> If NLP entails HDU, then very compelling arguments for HDU will need to be provided. Absent such arguments, the defender of THD is justified in resisting NLP.

Another issue of that same journal contains this comment on something another philosopher had said, "Although the statement that ... is probably misleading, it is nonetheless probably not inaccurate." Misleading, but not inaccurate?

Nothing could be more misleading than the use of initials for names and phrases as the LOL example shows. I don't know if people are in a hurry and don't want to take the time to write something out, if they think the use of initials makes them look learned, or if they are just plain lazy. For me, I think it is a mental disorder (MD) that the APA missed in DSM-V. Besides, I can't remember what the initials stand for, which is another type of disorder. Now, back to what I was talking about before.

Many psychologists who have studied DSM-V believe that well over 50% of the American population would qualify for one of the classifications or subtypes of mental disorders. If you add in the Internet disorders it approaches 99%. It has led to the slogan "Abnormal is the new normal." I'm not buying it. You might think that I do not appreciate the mental health sciences. Not so! The general public needs them in certain situations. But the need needs to be genuine and not created by broadening definitions. Remember I told you previously that I have taught psychology at the university level. I believe in its usefulness. It just seems that I have lived long enough to see the mental health sciences go crazy.

But I am not bitter about it. The classification of Post-Traumatic Embitterment Disorder (PTED) illustrates what I have been saying and brings us back on point. PTED is called the "Scrooge Syndrome." You remember from the movie what a bitter old man Scrooge was. He did not find his cure in therapy or pills. The cure for the poison of bitterness is to release people from any obligation for perceived hurts and to forgive them.

Forgiving

The cure for bitterness is forgiveness and you cannot overdose on it. If I am going to *carpe diem* and make the most of this day, I cannot be reliving past offenses against me. I must forgive and move on, looking forward and not back to what happened in the past.

We Christians look at forgiveness from a different perspective from those of other religions or no religion. We look at every offense we humans commit against one another as being an offense, a sin, against God. God made us in his image and he requires us to act as he would in every situation. To offend a fellow human being is a violation of God's commandment to love our neighbor as we love ourselves. Jesus' parable of the Good Samaritan illustrates that our neighbor can be any human being. When we look at the times we lived in denial and rebellion against the Person of God, and the times we have sinned against our fellow human beings, we see that our sins are great and innumerable. Yet, God took those sins and put them on His Son, Jesus Christ, on the cross. God can forgive our sins because Jesus bore the cost of our sins and died the death I should have died. When we look at all the sins against God we have been forgiven for, how could we not forgive a human being for one offense against us.

Here is how it works. To sin against God or our fellow man brings separation in the relationship and creates a debt on the books of the offender. In offering forgiveness of sins or offenses, it must be understood that forgiveness always costs someone something. If a financial debt is forgiven, it is cancelled and the one to whom the debt was owed absorbs the cost of the debt. If a visitor to your home breaks a valuable vase and you forgive the visitor, that means you absorb the loss of the cost of the vase and will not require the visitor to pay for it. If someone hurts your feelings and you forgive them, it means you will absorb the hurt and forego any retaliation. Christians believe that Jesus Christ absorbed the cost of our sins on the cross and restored our broken relationships with God. The object of forgiveness is reconciliation and peace with God and with each other.

Those who are not Christians have to will to forgive and there are good psychological reasons to do so (see, I'm not against psychology). I have already talked about the harmful psychological effects of bitterness and resentment brought on by unforgiveness. Forgiveness brings psychological benefits to the forgiver as well as to the one forgiven. Karl Menninger, the famed psychiatrist, once said that if he could convince the patients in psychiatric hospitals that their sins were forgiven, 75% of them could walk out the next day!

Studies show that just as unforgiveness has negative psychological effects, forgiveness brings positive effects to the mental and physical well-being of the one that forgives. Forgiveness can bring:

- Higher self-esteem
- Less anxiety and stress
- Absence of hostility
- Fewer symptoms of depression
- Lower blood pressure
- Stronger immune system
- Healthier and lasting relationships
- Overall better quality of life

So, why would someone not want to will to forgive and reap these benefits? Remember, if you don't practice forgiveness, you will be the one that pays most dearly.

There was an article published in *Psychology Today* magazine that shows that you could not just live better, but live longer by being willing to forgive. As was said, forgiveness is a choice and it will cost you the desire for revenge and the justified feelings of resentment. The research showed that if you make that choice you will probably live longer. The study was published in the *Journal of Behavioral Medicine* and used five categories of conditional and unconditional forgiveness. I want to mention two of them.

The study showed that respondents who believed in God's unconditional forgiveness (belief that God will forgive you, no matter what) had higher mortality rates than those that did not believe in God's unconditional forgiveness. The reason could be that they believed God would forgive them no matter what, so they felt the liberty to smoke, over eat and drink too much. It is also likely that if you believe in God's unconditional forgiveness you would be less likely to apologize and seek forgiveness from people you hurt, and therefore will have poor social relationships. These behavioral patterns lead to a statistically shorter life.

Another category that had a high mortality rate comprised those with a belief in conditional forgiveness of others. They felt they could not forgive unless the offender apologizes sincerely. Some even required the promise not to repeat the offending act before they could forgive it. The findings showed that people who make these demands for forgiveness continue to harbor resentment and hold on to grudges which can negatively affect the health of the heart, keeping stress levels high, breaking down the immune system and resulting in earlier death. The person who offends may not be available or willing to apologize. And they may not promise that it won't happen again.

Remember, forgiveness always costs something to somebody. If you are not willing to absorb the cost and let go of all requirements placed on the offender, then you will absorb another type of cost—a cost to your mental and physical health.

I don't want that, so I want to be the kind of old man who freely forgives.

As I said, forgiveness can and should lead to reconciliation in relationships. Now, my wife and I have a good relationship and we both are quick to forgive. In fact, my wife forgives me even when she is wrong. So do I!

There is a story of a father and son here in Spain who had become estranged in their relationship. The son ran away, and the father set off to find him. He searched for months to no avail. Finally, in a last desperate effort to find him, the father put an ad in the Madrid newspaper. The ad read: "Dear Paco, meet me in front of this newspaper office at noon on Saturday. All is forgiven. I love you, Your Father." On Saturday, over 800 Pacos showed up, looking for forgiveness and love from their father. That story says it all. If the hurts involve someone whose relationship you otherwise value, forgiveness can and should lead to reconciliation.

When Pánfilo de Narváez, the Spanish conquistador, lay dying, his father-confessor asked him whether he had forgiven all his enemies. Narvaez looked astonished and said, "Father, I have no enemies, I have shot them all." That is not what I mean. You cannot be reconciled to people you have killed.

Reconciliation is not possible in all cases. Perhaps the offender has died. Or perhaps the offender refuses to communicate with you and does not value the relationship as you do. Still, forgiveness is possible, beneficial and necessary for one's own well-being even if reconciliation is not possible.

Forgiveness and doing all you can to restore relationships brings peace to the soul. It is impossible to *carpe diem* and live a life of peace if there is unforgiveness present today. Psychologist Lewis Smedes said, "You will know that forgiveness has begun when you recall those who hurt you and feel the power to wish them well." If I am going to be the kind of old man I want to be, that is how I must be today.

Humble

If I am going to be the kind of old man who people want to be around, I must be humble. That is another word that probably has as many definitions as there are people claiming to be it. I think the best place to start in seeking the real meaning of a word is in its ethnology. Humble comes through the Middle English from Old French, which was from the Latin *humilis* meaning "low, lowly" which was derived from *humus* meaning "ground or dirt." In looking at definitions that apply to oneself, to be humble does not mean to think of yourself as being dirt. The psychologists would not like that. Rather, it means "not proud" or not thinking of yourself as better than other people, even the lowest of society. It means that we can look on other people, no matter their situation, and say, "There, but for the grace of God, go I."

Confucius said that humility is the solid foundation of all virtues. I have to agree with that. Who appreciates the generosity of an arrogant man? Whatever virtues I may have will not endear me to people if I do not carry them as a humble man. When I think about a future dependent upon my wife or strangers in a care home, it does humble me. The German divine Thomas à Kempis said, "A true understanding and humble estimate of oneself is the highest and most valuable of all lessons. To take no account of oneself, but always to think well and highly of others is the highest wisdom and perfection." If I could do that, would you like me?

As with other things we have discussed, there are psychological advantages to being humble. Interestingly enough, the words humble and humility do not appear in most psychology dictionaries. The personality traits opposite to humble have been studied and classified robustly in social psychology. These include aggressive, self-enhancement, egocentric, narcissistic, and arrogant. These traits are affirmed in self-help books teaching that self-assertion is the only way to get ahead in the world. It may help in the short term but being that way will not cause you to be well-liked. People who assert themselves should keep in mind what the French philosopher Michel de Montaigne said, "On the highest throne in the world, we still sit only on our bottom." In other words, as Charles Spurgeon said, "The best men are conscious, above all others, that they are men at best." We are all human beings that sit on our bottoms and to be well-liked we need to like others more than we like ourselves.

I'm sorry, back to the psychological benefits of being humble. Maybe the reason there has not been more study on it is because it is hard to measure in a person. According to a report published in *Observer*, the journal of the Association for Psychological Science, titled, "Measuring Humility and Its Positive Effects," the measurement of humility is "shrouded in paradox. Someone who claims to be 'very humble' on a self-report measure might be displaying arrogance and lack of awareness." People do brag about being humble. The report states that defining humility involves an accurate view of the self and "a stance that is other-oriented rather than self-focused." This echoes what the Bible commands for Christians: "Do not think of yourself more highly than you ought, but rather think of yourself with sober judgment" (Romans 12:3); and, "Do nothing out of selfish ambition or vain conceit, but in humility consider others better than yourselves" (Philippians 2:3). That is the kind of old man I want to be.

Humility strengthens social bonds, especially important relationships that might experience conflict or difference of opinion. My wife is aware of this and therefore she always does the humble thing: she admits it when I am wrong. Humility is like forgiveness in a relationship; it greases the wheels and makes it roll along smoothly. The wear-and-tear that plagues relationships where differences of opinion exist is buffered by humility—considering others more highly than yourself. Giving the other person the benefit of the doubt considering that they just might be right will strengthen the relationship. Relationships between humble people do not produce much stress in a person's life. As we have seen before, stress is a major cause of physical and mental health issues. Humility helps keep stress to the minimum and health to the maximum.

The first rule to being humble is we err greatly if we get our opinion of ourselves from our dog. If you are a married man, the wife might be a better place to start. When my wife and I got married, we were both Christians, but we did have one big religious difference—I thought I was God, she did not. She has subsequently made me see that she was right. When humility escapes me, she reminds me that when we got married men were like parking places, the good ones were already taken and the ones available were handicapped or too small. That will keep me humble. If she thinks I might be tempted to take any pride in the way I look, she reminds me that she sees me when I wake up in the morning. And I humbly thank God for her.

Speaking of God, the perfect example of a humble person, one that really exemplifies the trait of humility, is Jesus Christ. God became man; the greatest became the least. And he willingly did it. His humility is described in Philippians 2:6–8 in the Bible:

> 6 Who, being in very nature God, did not consider equality with God something to be grasped,
>
> 7 but made himself nothing, taking the very nature of a servant ,being made in human likeness.
>
> 8 And being found in appearance as a man, he humbled himself and became obedient to death—even death on a cross!

To set aside his glory and take the form of a man and to suffer like a fellowman is true humility. He did not think of himself; he thought of us. In the words of C.S. Lewis, "True humility is not thinking less of yourself; it is thinking of yourself less." That is how Jesus was. That is how I want to be. If I am going to *carpe diem*, make the most of this day, I must be an old man who makes the least of himself. I need to be humble today.

No complaining

If I am going to *carpe diem*, that is, to make the most of every day, I need to stay on the positive side of negative. In other words, instead of complaining about a glass being half empty, I need to see it as half full with the potential of holding the same amount again. Who wants to be around a grumbling, complaining old man? I don't! And I don't want to be one. I want to wag more and bark less.

Remember, I want to be an old man who is fun to be around. I don't know what my future holds. If I suffer physically, I hope I can do it without complaining. You have probably heard of Stephen Hawking, the English theoretical physicist, whose career has made him famous with his succession of bold statements about cosmology followed several years later by retractions and new theories. That's OK; that's what scientists do.

I bring him up here because he has amyotrophic lateral sclerosis, which has left him paralyzed and only able to communicate by using a single cheek muscle attached to a speech generating device. I don't care how famous you are, that is a hard life. He's in his 70's now and if he was a grumbling, complaining old man he would not be listened to. But he is not. With all his learning, he says this is the most useful thing he has learned, "People won't have time for you if you are always angry or complaining." That is not theory; that is fact.

Psychologists (here we go again with psychology) have determined that complaining damages one's mental health. According to an article in *Psychology Today*, we complain because we are frustrated and we repeat the same tales of woe to everyone we talk to in an effort to relieve ourselves of that frustration. Complaining about things you cannot do anything about leaves you feeling helpless and hopeless. The accumulation of frustration and helplessness over time affects our self-esteem, mood, our mental health, and eventually our physical health.

Other psychologists report that the more we complain, the more unhappy we get. They use the term "negative bias" to refer to the psychological phenomenon of the human tendency to focus more on the negative than the positive. Studies have proved that the brain's reaction to negative stimuli is much more intense than it is to positive stimuli. We are more likely to focus on and remember negative things that happen to us than we are on the positive. That could be a good thing when the negative thing is something that needs to be addressed in our lives and something we can do something about. When we can't do anything about it, it creates frustration. Then we use complaining as a coping mechanism.

Because I still do it, I know that complaining can have some positive effects. But I have also found out that those positive effects are short-lived and counter-productive. One benefit of complaining is that it keeps you at the center of attention as you are the one doing the talking. It also seems to let you off the hook as far as being responsible. If you complain about it, it must not be your fault. Another benefit is that it is a good conversation starter. Since people tend to focus on the negative, they like to talk about negative things, tending to try to come up with a bigger complaint than yours. Complaining is contagious and before long everybody is sick of it. If I am that kind of old man, as Stephen Hawkins said, people will not have time for me.

So, how do I keep from being a negative, complaining old man? I need to think, see, and speak positive. Every day is a good day. If you don't believe it, try missing one. Abraham Lincoln said, "Most folks are about as happy as they make up their minds to be." There was a song written by Roger Miller back in the 1960's that included these lines, "You can't roller skate in a buffalo herd, but you can be happy if you've a mind to." As I get older, I need to acknowledge that there are some things that I just cannot do (either I cannot do them anymore or I may never get to do them), but I can make up my mind to be happy and content with the things I still can do. I need to have a positive attitude about the life I have left.

You guessed it! There are psychological benefits of keeping a positive mental attitude. Empirical research has found that there are very real health benefits linked to having a positive mental attitude (PMA). According to The Mayo Clinic website, positive thinking is linked to:

- Longer life span
- Less stress
- Lower rates of depression

- Increased resistance to sickness
- Better stress management and coping skills
- Lower risk of heart disease
- Increased physical well-being
- Better psychological health

One study found that adults with a PMA could reduce frailty during old age. Other research has found that our thoughts and attitudes have an effect on our immune system. The findings show that negative thoughts and emotions lead to weaker immunity to the onset of colds and flu. All the more reason that I want to keep a PMA.

If you look for a positive side of things, you can usually find one. I don't really know what kind of old man Albert Einstein was, other than smart, but I do know he showed a PMA when he said, "In the middle of difficulty lies opportunity." There is always an opportunity to be kind and always an opportunity to think kind thoughts. I heard somebody say, "When someone calls me ugly, I feel sorry for them. Life must be hard for the visually impaired." Thinking positive means remembering that you are unique and special, just like everybody else. Thinking positive is when someone asked me if I could fly an aerobatics plane like my wife and I responded, "I don't know, I haven't tried."

Yes, I want to be the kind of old man who lives in the present, is current, content, grateful, without bitterness, forgiving, humble, does not complain and has a positive mental attitude, and who makes the most of every day. Remember:

> Every day is special. You have never seen it before.
> You will never see it again.
> ❋ *Carpe Diem* ❋

[5]
Life: The Rest of the Story

"When you arise in the morning,
think of what a precious privilege it is to be
alive—to breathe, to think, to enjoy, to love."
—Marcus Aurelius

THE REST OF THE STORY was a Monday-through-Friday radio program originally hosted by Paul Harvey. He became the most listened to man in the history of radio. Beginning as a part of his newscasts during World War II and then premiering as its own series on the ABC Radio Networks on May 10, 1976, *The Rest of the Story* consisted of stories presented on a variety of subjects with some key surprise element of the story held back until the end. The broadcasts always concluded with the tag line "And now you know the rest of the story."

As a man in his late 60's, I realize that I am writing the rest of my story and I need to give some thought to how it is going to end. Statistically, I only have about 15 years of reasonable health and mobility left in which to finish my life story. After that, if I am still alive, it will only be a matter of reliving it and re-telling it until I can't remember it any longer. The important thing for me is to do what Marcus Aurelius said above, and to do what I said in Chapter 4, that is, *carpe diem*, and remember that today is one page in the rest of my story. I need to write it like I want it to read, keeping in mind the reality of my situation.

Declining years

The reality of my situation is that I am in what is called my declining years. When people say that, they generally mean that one's health and mobility are declining and that every year brings more aches and pains and sees more physical activities cease. The dictionary definition of declining years is the time leading up to something's demise; a time of increasing ineffectiveness (why didn't it say decreasing effectiveness?). That is certainly one take on the subject.

In his book, *Old Age and How to Survive It*, Edward Enfield gives another meaning to it. He defines declining years thus: "This is the period in which you decline to do anything you don't feel like doing." He goes on to state, "One of the great delights of the Declining Years is that the list of things you don't have to do is constantly expanding." It is true that old people have a built-in excuse for declining to do things: "My arthritis is acting up," "I have a doctor's appointment that day," or, "The grandkids are coming." What Enfield is talking about is being at a time of life when you have the freedom to choose what you do and who you want to do it with. You are no longer trying to get ahead so you no longer have to tolerate intolerable people. You are not trying to impress anybody so you don't have to do things that are not needful and that you would not enjoy. There is freedom in that.

My wife and I have kind of adopted that view of our declining years. We are still working as Christian missionaries doing what God has called us to do and we are enjoying it more because we no longer put pressure on ourselves to go and do when we don't feel like it. God is not a hard taskmaster and he has cut us some slack in our declining years. That does not mean we are doing less, it means we are doing it because we want to and we are enjoying it more.

We are now living in Spain. The Spaniards, unlike people any place else we have lived, are late night people. If you get invited to someone's home for dinner, you go about 8:30 PM and eat about 10:00 PM and leave about midnight. We are not late night people. We eat dinner about 6 PM and *mi cama me llama* (my bed calls me) about 10:30 PM. We find ourselves declining more and more dinner invitations. Lunch works better for us.

One aspect of most people's view of our declining years is the belief that people's minds begin to decline after age 60. Declines—yes; begins to—no! A recent study published in the *British Medical Journal* reported that if you are 45 or older I may need to write this a little slower for you because cognitive decline begins about then. Over 7,000 people were analyzed over a 10-year period and, sure enough, that's what they found. But before you 45–60 year olds become alarmed, I need to inform you that the population studied was biased—all the subjects were British civil servants. That might be an unscientific explanation for the findings of cognitive decline.

Many old people, like authors, composers and painters, are able to keep doing in their old age what they did throughout their adult lives. Their activities do not decline. They continue to do it because they enjoy it. Other old people are forced to retire from their work and are forced to fill their time with new activities. Unfortunately, for many their time is filled with watching TV and walking the dog. Others are pro-active and look for new challenges in life. Some are writing the rest of their story as if it was just starting. Here are a few examples that inspire me:

> Kimani Maruge – enrolled in the first grade of primary school at age 84.
> Mohr Keet – decided to bungee jump at age 96.
> Dorothy Davenhill Hirsch – decided to visit the North Pole at age 89.
> Gladys Burrell – completed a marathon at age 92.
> James C. Warren – obtained his first pilot's license at age 87.
> Nola Ochs – graduated from college at age 95.
> Edythe Karchmaier – became the oldest registered Facebook user at age 107.

So you see, the declining years do not have to be written with a downward slope as if you are over the hill and going down for the rest of your life.

There can be some surprise elements to be written in the rest of my story. What they are, I do not know as yet. I do know that with God all things are possible (Matthew 19:26). That adds a great deal of excitement to my declining years.

I do not profess to be a lover of poetry, especially modern poetry, and will not become one in my declining years. My definition of poetry is: when someone that does not have something to say, says it anyway—that is poetry. Poets are like philosophers, in that it is hard to find a happy one. Typical of modern poetry websites is spharnx.com. The contributors to this site certainly do not write happy poems and I think it is because they do not believe in anything, thus they express thoughts in the negative. There is a poem posted titled "It's Me" and states in part: "It's me. I'm still here. Still think the same...I think wrong way. Oh well, I have my beliefs." Hardly Robert Frost or Emily Dickinson. Oh well, I have my beliefs, too, and I believe that I will decline to read modern poetry in my declining years. That site does have this poetic take on declining years:

> The Poetry of Declining Years
> By spharnx
>
> The poet is declining.
> Getting older.
> Poems lie around
> Not finished,
> Incomplete,
> Not keypunched,
> Not filed,
> Not saved,
> Not recited,
> Not heard,
> Not read,
> Not known.
>
> No matter.
> What of it?

I personally do not want to leave any unfinished poems or unfinished business when I die. I do not want to have any regrets for things undone that could have been done in my declining years.

No regrets

I enjoy living with my wife, I enjoy living with my Spanish neighbors, but I do not enjoy living with regrets. Therefore, I want to be the kind of old man who has dealt with his regrets and has moved on.

The area of regret can cover a multitude of sins; sins of omission and sins of commission. First, I want to talk about the sins of omission, that is, the things I did not do and the places I did not see that I could regret not doing or seeing.

Old people like to sit around and talk about "what might have been"; "if only I had..."; "woulda-coulda-shoulda." Missed opportunities and making wrong choices haunt our memories and make us miss current opportunities. Alexander Graham Bell had a good understanding of the negative effect of regret: "When one door closes, another opens; but we often look so long and so regretfully upon the closed door that we do not see the one that has opened for us." Yes, one negative effect of living with regrets is the missed opportunities we do not see because we are still looking at the one we blew. Believe me, I have blown a lot.

On a side note here, there is one thing that I am glad I do not have to regret—I am glad I do not have to regret getting a tattoo because I never got one. Nursing homes enter my thinking more than they used to and I can just imagine the scene 40 to 50 years from now. The residents are sitting around looking at faded tattoos wondering what that stuff is on their skin and why won't it wash off. But that is for you younger people to think about, us oldies don't have to.

Many famous people lived with regret and it was reflected in their lives and work. Here is a sample of their conclusions:

"Youth is a blunder; Manhood a struggle; Old Age a regret."
—Benjamin Disraeli

"Droll thing life is—that mysterious arrangement of merciless logic for a futile purpose. The most you can hope from it is some knowledge of yourself—that comes too late—a crop of inextinguishable regrets"
—Joseph Conrad

"No, I regret nothing, all I regret is having been born; dying is such a long tiresome business I always found."
—Samuel Beckett

"I see it all perfectly; there are two possible situations—one can either do this or that. My honest opinion and my friendly advice is this; do it or do not do it—you will regret both."
—Soren Kierkegaard

Disraeli was a British politician who had some successes but spent most of his political career in an opposition party. Politicians should have lots of regrets. Conrad and Beckett were writers whose lives ... well they can be excused. And Kierkegaard was a philosopher, which explains why everything for him leads to regret.

Regrets arise from doing something that is perceived to be the wrong thing to do or from not doing what would have been the better or right thing to do. From that standpoint, Kierkegaard was right, in that doing and not doing leads to regrets. And I am sure you have anticipated this—there are psychological effects that come with regret. I want to deal with this a bit because we old people have had a long time to make the wrong mistakes (as Yogi says), and accumulate a lot of regrets. According to psychologists that is not good for us.

The *Psychology Today* website posted an article a couple of years ago titled "The Psychology of Regret." It stated, "Regret is a negative cognitive/emotional state that involves blaming ourselves for a bad outcome, feeling a sense of loss or sorrow at what might have been or wishing we could undo a previous choice that we made." Regret can be a positive factor in helping us make a better choice next time when the situation dictates a second chance. However, with most regrets the damage is done and cannot be corrected. If that is the case, "The more likely it is that regret can turn into rumination and chronic stress that damages mind and body." When that happens, depression is not far behind.

Research shows that in the short run people tend to regret actions taken and mistakes made (sins of commission). Over long periods of time, which us oldies have behind us, people are more likely to regret actions not taken and opportunities missed (sins of omission). We cannot go back in time and change decisions made and words spoken and that can lead to feelings of helplessness and make us hesitant to make decisions that we currently need to make.

The *Personality and Social Psychology Bulletin* published research showing that inaction regrets (missing opportunities) lasted longer than action regrets (making perceived wrong decisions), and the inaction regrets resulted in a more acute sense of loss. The inaction or loss of opportunity makes the person look bad as if it was their fault because they could have done something and they did not. Likewise, regret feelings tend to last longer if a second chance to do what you did not do still exists. The person feels regret as long as the opportunity is still open. This explains why education is the number one regret of Americans in all age and social levels. As Kimani Maruge showed, you can always enroll in school. By the way, two thru five of the top five biggest regrets in life centered on career, romance, parenting and self.

Another journal, called *Organizational Behavior and Human Decision Processes*, published a study on how regret aversion affects decision-making. The research showed anticipated regret weighs heavier than anticipated joy when making a decision. After the decision is made, people prefer to avoid information that might cause them to regret their decision and they seek information that reinforces it. That is so they can avoid what psychologists call cognitive dissonance, which is defined as the feeling of discomfort that results from holding two conflicting beliefs. The marketing professionals use advertising to get the most advantage out of people's cognitive dissonance. They want you to feel good that you bought their product and bad if you bought a competitor's product.

I'll give you an example of how that works in an old person's life. In my efforts to be an old man who stays current, I just bought my wife and myself a couple of eBook readers. The brand I was looking at offered two models that looked the same and had almost the same features but one costs almost 60% more than the other. Guess which one I bought—right, the more expensive one. The reason I did that was because I did not want to regret in the future not buying the more expensive one. I would have been happy with the less expensive one, but I would probably think I would have been happier with the more expensive one and would always regret not buying it. They both would have served the purpose, but I HAVE to believe that the one I bought was the right choice.

That is how regret aversion works and subconsciously is the driving force behind a lot of the decisions we old folks make.

We don't have time to live with regret. If you want to read some sad stuff, do an Internet search on deathbed regrets. Now is the time for us seniors to *carpe diem* and deal with our regrets.

I became a Christian when I was 38 years old. For the last 20 of those years I had lived a selfish, self-centered life and had done and said some things that I really regretted. After becoming a Christian, and realizing how much I had sinned against God and that all of that was put right by Jesus' death on the cross, I set about to put things right with my fellowman so that I would not have regrets. Where it was at all possible, I sought out people I had wronged in word or deed and apologized, keeping in mind the words of Benjamin Franklin, "Never ruin an apology with an excuse." I cannot tell you how much better I felt after completing that task. For me, regret for things done in the past is past—*carpe diem*. Eleanor Roosevelt left some good advice for regret avoidance in relationships: "One of the blessings of age is to learn not to part on a note of sharpness, to treasure the moments spent with those we love, and to make them whenever possible good to remember, for time is short."

Failures

One thing the philosopher Kierkegaard got right was this bit of wisdom: "Life must be understood backward. But it must be lived forward." Looking back on past failures and dwelling there is one way to keep from living life forward. Sure, failures have happened in everyone's past, but they should be stepping stones rather than tombstones. People do not learn nearly as much by succeeding as they do by failing if the right attitude is adopted. I heard one guy say, "I don't fail, I succeed in finding what does not work." The great inventor Thomas Edison said, "I have not failed ... I've just found 10,000 ways that won't work." Another one said, "I tried to fail and succeeded." As I have gotten older, I have tried to adopt an attitude of learning from my failures and I expect to learn a lot today.

My father gave us boys some good advice by telling us that no matter what we chose to do, if we do it the best we can, we may not succeed, but we will not be failures. I have tried to live my life that way and have done my best. Unfortunately, I was doing my best when I was doing my worst and accomplished some things that I am not proud of now. So, now I only do what I can be proud of if I succeed. As I write the rest of my story, I am trying to live my life forward keeping in mind the words of former US Vice President Dan Quayle, "If we don't succeed, we run the risk of failure."

My wife is one who has succeeded in a lot of things. She has done things your average woman would not even consider, much less attempt. But there is one thing that she has not succeeded in; in fact, she is an utter failure. She loves to shop. When we go walking around town, if I don't hold her hand she goes shopping. She has been a shopper for all the years I have known her. Yet, after all these years, she still does not have a thing to wear. Could it be that in failing she is succeeding?

I, on the other hand, have failed at many things. In my young adult life I was athletic. I tried to become a professional tennis player, but failed. I tried to get around a golf course in less than 80 strokes, but failed. In recent years I have failed to stay in good athletic shape and that I do regret. I am in shape; round's a shape. It's just that being overweight 24 hours a day fits my schedule better than exercising one hour a day. When it comes to exercise for exercise sake, my philosophy is: No pain, no pain. However, I do get exercise. I do pull-ups (to the table) and forklifts at least three times a day. Exercise seems to come with old age. I find myself exercising caution more. And I am experiencing what Virginia Ironsides said, "I can't remember where I put things, but I get a lot of exercise looking for them." For us older folks, exercise happens.

Speaking of being in shape, since we have been living in Europe I have complained about the shape of the men's clothes they sell in the stores. Men's clothes in Europe come only in size 2 (i.e. 2 short or 2 tight). They are designed for people shaped like an hourglass and I am shaped like a clock. I know I have not stopped growing, however, now it is horizontally rather than vertically. But still, I fail at shopping but it is not my fault. Speaking of not my fault, I love to blame things on the computer these days. Us old men like scapegoats to keep us from looking like failures.

Here is one more thought for old men about failures. Maybe we did not accomplish everything that we have always dreamed of doing, but that does not mean that, in old age, we quit trying. I ran across this good advice the other day: "Never give up on your dreams, keep sleeping."

OK, here is one more one more thought (this habit seems to be habitual with me). Being older should not keep us from trying to improve ourselves even though we do run the risk of more failures. Don't let the failure be in not trying, rather than in not succeeding. As a young adult I did not read anything that was not work related and I watched television a lot. Remember, I told you before that we do not watch television now, we are readers. Since becoming a reader I have found that my reading skills have improved. I was recently tested and at 68 years old I am reading at a 70.5-year-old level. Man! I am proud of that and I feel like a success. Oh well! Enough of this. Have I succeeded in writing about failures in my old age? I was told to always write with the reading public in mind and I am thinking about you right now.

Legacy

This chapter is about me writing the rest of my story and how I want it to read. Leaving a legacy has to do with how my story is going to read after I have reached the end of the story and am six feet under. When I leave, what will I leave? The legal side of legacy has to do with money and personal property bequeathed to someone in my will. If you own anything, it is important to get this aspect of legacy in order before your story is finished. For us oldies that would be the sooner the better. The personal side of legacy has to do with a heritage passed on, or more specifically, what people will remember about me after I am gone. I want to be the kind of old man who leaves a good legacy.

I read a little devotional each morning out of a book called *Thoughts for the Quiet Hour*. It gives a Scripture verse and a few thoughts on that verse for every day of the year. I always get a not so subtle reminder every year on my birthday. The verse for my birthday is James 4:14, which says, "What is your life? You are a mist that appears for a little while and then vanishes." My concern is whether or not my mist will be missed when I vanish.

Acha atoma katika dunia baada kuondoka means "leave a mark on the world after leaving" in Swahili. In my declining years, when some activities are ceasing, I have been thinking about what kind of mark I am leaving on my world; my legacy, so to speak. I am reminded that I am making that mark now by the words of author Dillion Burroughs when he advised, "Live today the way you want to be remembered tomorrow."

By the time they get old, some people have accumulated a lot of wealth and they can leave behind tangible things for which they will be remembered. Hospitals, libraries and university buildings are some things that are named after people who donated the money to build them. Their names will be known long after they are dead, but the people themselves, the kind of people they were, will not be known unless they leave something else besides bricks and mortar. Since I do not have bricks and mortar, nor the resources to buy them, I must be concerned with a different kind of legacy. I must do something that will live after I am dead; something that says Jack was here in the years xxxx to xxxx. Leaving children leaves progeny, but does not necessarily leave a legacy. Your legacy keeps your DNA; your progeny mixes it.

Sometime back in the 1980's, I attended a seminar featuring the late motivational speaker Charles "Tremendous" Jones. His mantra was, "Remember, you are the same today as you'll be five years from now, except for two things: the people you meet and the books you read. Choose both carefully." He wrote a book titled *Life is Tremendous* among many others. His books sold in the millions. Most of all, Jones is remembered for the kind of person he was. His legacy in people's lives is reflected in their comments: "Charlie lit warm fires in cold rooms"; "Charlie spoke life into me"; "I wish I had met him 20 years ago"; "He was Great and Humble"; "They don't call him 'Tremendous' for nothing!" Now that is a legacy!

OK, so what does the legacy of "Tremendous" have to do with my desire to leave a legacy? Charlie lived his mantra. People's lives were changed when they met him and when they read his books. I am making a humble attempt to write some books that hopefully will live on after me. But I would rather be remembered for being the kind of old man who "lit warm fires in cold rooms." Charles "Tremendous" Jones was a mensch and I want to be remembered for being one, too.

A mensch

Mensch is a Yiddish word. Leo Rosten's *The Joys of Yiddish* says, "A mensch is a someone to admire and emulate, someone of noble character. The key to being a 'real mensch' is nothing less than character, rectitude, dignity, a sense of what is right, responsible, decorous." That is a tall order and that is what I want to be remembered as being. Therefore, that is the kind of old man I want to be now. Who says you have to be dead to leave a legacy?

For me to be a mensch now, I need to be a superman. Besides the qualities listed above, a mensch is honorable, caring, truthful, safe, and looks for opportunities to do good. Those qualities must be reflected in one's response to hardship and disappointments, the way one treats other people, and one's use of money, powers and authority. There is only one superman who ever lived, only one man who was a true mensch—Jesus Christ. As a Christian, I want to be like him. The Bible says "he was without sin"; "he went around doing good"; and, "he did not come to be served, but to serve." In the end, "he gave his life for a ransom for many." That's a real mensch!

A spiritual legacy

I hope and pray people will be blessed by reading my books. And I hope and pray people will be blessed by knowing me. Those blessings will last for a while, but they will not last forever. The spiritual legacy I want to leave will come from introducing people to Jesus Christ as their Lord and Savior. We

Christians believe that is an eternal blessing. That has been our life work as missionaries—to introduce people to Jesus Christ. He is more tremendous than "Tremendous" Jones. Jones only brought warmth to cold rooms. Jesus brings warmth to cold hearts. The two disciples on the road to Emmaus met him. Their testimony was, "Were not our hearts burning within us while he talked with us on the road and opened the Scriptures to us?" To know Jesus Christ, that is the kind of spiritual legacy I want to leave and I want to be the kind of old man mensch that leaves that legacy.

As I am writing the rest of my story in these declining years of my life, I want my remaining years to be joyful and fruitful. I leave this chapter with some wise words:

> "And in the end, it's not the years in your life that counts.
> It's the life in your years."
> —Abraham Lincoln

[6]

Life: The End of the Story

> "I am not afraid of death;
> I just don't want to be there when it happens."
> —Woody Allen

OL' WOODY IS PRETTY CLEVER in some things and pretty naive in others. As you know, he is a film star and a film director of much repute. He lives for fantasy on the big screen and it has left him out of touch with reality. If you read his interviews and see his movies, you are left wondering if a real Woody Allen exists. But we know a real Woody Allen does exist and the real Woody Allen will one day face the reality of his own death—and he will be there when it happens.

Now, I am not going to give you a lot of statistics on death, but I could. I do know that too many birthdays will kill you. More people die of death than any other cause. The only statistic that concerns me is that death kills over 2.5 million Americans every year and one year I will be part of that statistic. I want to be the kind of old man who is ready for death in case my year is this year.

The reality of death has been on the mind of man since the beginning of human history. Probably the oldest writing that exists on the subject is the ancient Egyptian *Book of the Dead*, with some parts dating from 2400 BC. The texts are made up of spells and magic formulas and physical objects placed in tombs and believed to protect and help the dead person in the hereafter. In the Torah of the Jewish faith and in Christian scriptures, it is recorded that death entered the human reality because of sin, and that happened to the first human beings that we have a record of. Paul Tournier was a Swiss psychologist and medical doctor who faced his own death in 1986. He wrote a book titled *Learn to Grown Old*. He points out that death is a part of old age and it is imperative that one gets ready for it. He writes, "We have a choice. We can face the reality of death or we can evade it. But we cannot avoid the reality of death."

Once we reach a responsible adulthood, the specter of death is always there. For some it is a distant shadow. For others it is an ever-present possibility. With the high incidence of cancer in the world today, and with no cure being available to date, every new pain could be a symptom of that hidden killer. It has been for millions, and it can strike at any age; all the more reason to deal with the eventuality while you can.

Death is coming and we err to deny it. Tournier said, "One may indeed pull out the odd white hair. That is quite all right provided we do not lie to ourselves." Old age is leading to death and the older we get the faster it gallops toward us, i.e., the faster our remaining life seems to be passing. The British author and screenwriter John Mortimer compared his life to the scriptwriter's pace, "scenes get shorter and the action speeds up towards the end." Remember the learned Andy Rooney? I've shared with you previously some of the things he learned before he died. He said, "I have learned that life is like a roll of toilet paper. The closer it gets to the end, the faster it goes."

Death is coming and we need to be comfortable with that fact. The majority of people alive are not. The philosopher Marcus Aurelius wrote, "The act of dying is one of the acts of life." The majority of people do not want the play to end. The late American humanist, scientist and author Isaac Asimov wrote, "Life is pleasant. Death is peaceful. It's the transition that's troublesome." The act of dying, the process of death, may be brief or long. Many people think they would not mind being dead (out of their misery) but they do not want to suffer during the transition from life to death.

Do you see that there are two things involved in dealing with one's own death? There is the process of dying and there is the final state of death. Both bring fear to people. The television comedian George Burns, said, "At my age flowers scare me." The National Institute of Mental Health did some research in 2014 on people's fears and worries. Necrophobia, the fear of death, was the number two fear people expressed. Oddly enough, the number one fear people expressed was the fear of public speaking. That prompted the comedian Jerry Seinfeld to point out that when you go to a funeral the people attending are more afraid of being the one to do the eulogy than they are of being the one in the casket. That reminds me of another thing Yogi Berra said. He advised, "Always go to other people's funerals; otherwise they won't go to yours."

I want to deal with the process of dying first, and will deal with the final state of death later in this chapter. The advances of medical science have prolonged diseased life. When that happens, the possibilities for a gentle closure to one's life is often replaced by overwhelming physical pain. And that is what people fear the most in the dying process. British author and philosopher Aldous Huxley wrote, "Ignore death up to the last moment; then, when it can't be ignored any longer, have yourself squirted full of morphia and shuffle off in a coma. Thoroughly sensible, humane and scientific, eh?" Huxley died of laryngeal cancer in 1963 and followed his own advice, except he used LSD rather than morphia to shuffle off with.

Help to die

Huxley was a prophet in that he described the way people in pain prefer to die today. Two medical fields have evolved from Huxley's path through the process of dying. Thanatology is the scientific study of death. The word is derived from the Greek language. In Greek mythology, Thanatos is the personification of death. The suffix *logia*, means the "study of." Books started appearing on the subject around the time of Huxley's death. Death had long been a subject for philosophy and literature. Now it is a division of scientific study.

Another medical field that has developed since Huxley's death is palliative care. This is specialized medical care for people with serious and usually incurable diseases. Palliative comes from the Latin, *palliare*, meaning "to cloak." It focuses on providing patients with relief from the symptoms, pain, physical stress, and mental stress of serious illness—whatever the diagnosis. The term is usually used to mean noncurative therapy. The treatments are said to have palliative (relieving) effect if they relieve symptoms without having a curative effect on the underlying disease or cause. Of course, this means the use of morphine to relieve pain. The primary provider of palliative care in the US is the Hospice Organization. Their primary means of relieving pain for patients who are dying is the use of morphine. According to their website, they provide services to over 1.5 million people a year. Remember the statistic of 2.5 million people dying in the US each year and you can see the magnitude of fear of the dying process.

Palliative care has morphed into another area of the dying process. Assisted suicide is suicide committed with the aid of another person, sometimes a physician. Yes, doctors are, says one article, "knowingly and intentionally providing a person with the knowledge or means or both required to commit suicide, including counseling about lethal doses of drugs, prescribing such lethal doses or supplying the drugs." Technically, the physician can only prescribe lethal medication in jurisdictions where it is legal.

Many countries in Europe and states in the US have legalized assisted suicide. The Statement of Marbella was adopted by the World Medical Assembly right here in Spain in 1992. It calls for physicians to respect the autonomy of patients, meaning that a physician is to respect that "food or treatment refusal is the individual's choice." It defines the "benefit" of individuals to include respecting their wishes and not forcing treatment. To benefit does not necessarily involve prolonging life at all costs. We now see this played out in living wills and the patient's own decision to unplug life-support systems. A friend of mine told me he and his wife were discussing a living will and he told her that if he ever got dependent on a machine and liquids to live he wanted her to stop it. She said, "OK, Dear." So got up and unplugged the TV and poured out his cup of coffee. But, you get my point here, don't you? People do not want pain in the death process, and whole industries and many governments are making it so they do not have to. It is amazing, how many people who did not do a good job of controlling their lives want to control their deaths.

What? My wife just came in and said I need to get an electric guitar or a haircut. So I'm off to get a haircut. I leave you to ponder society's willingness to help you die from a philosophical standpoint. Why is this thus? What is the meaning of this thus-ness?

...OK, I'm back. Did you get it figured out? Or were you pondering the deeper philosophical question of the is-ness of nothing-ness?

Back to reality, here is something else for you to think about.

My time is coming

Ecclesiastes 3 starts out: "There is a time for everything, and a season for every activity under heaven. A time to be born and a time to die." No doubt, my time is coming. The biggest end-of-life issue is: will I be ready when death comes? From a psychological standpoint I am ready, and I have a good reason for it. I was born in 1946. Now consider what has happened since then.

1951 – First science fiction film. Today most of what was portrayed in those early
films are no longer fiction, but reality.

1952 – First Rock and Roll concert. Today that music is free in every store, restaurant and most churches. When I leave home I cannot get away from it.

1954 – Television became available for most middle-income families. Before television in the home, families talked to each other. Radio dramas were popular. People, especially children, had to use their imagination to picture the action as they listened. Today, television visualizes everything, leaving nothing to the imagination, and has really dumbed down the public.

1956 – Interstate highways appeared. Before that, travelling long distances in a car could take days, thus taking days out of a vacation, or adding days to a business trip. A trip of 1,000 miles could take three days. Today that distance could be travelled in 18 hours and can be done safely if there are two drivers.

1957 – Space travel began. Today, men have walked on the moon, and people are living on space platforms. (I still haven't figured out why.)

1960 – First birth-control pill. Sex without consequence has become the norm.

1964 – The Civil Rights Act was passed. Before this, black and white races lived separately in society. Today it is against the law to discriminate against anybody for anything.

1973 – Roe v. Wade legalized abortion. Before that, life in the womb had value and was protected by law. Today, the unborn is considered to be a malignant growth that can be easily disposed of. Abortion has been relegated to a religious issue and is no longer a moral issue in secular society.

1993 – The Internet came online. Need I say more?

Beginning in the 1950's, the medical field has made huge advances in treatment of illnesses. Vaccines against polio, measles and rubella have almost wiped out those diseases. There are now drugs to successfully treat tuberculosis, which used to be a killer. Organ transplants, including the heart, began in the 1960's, thus extending the lives of many.

Since the 1950's, DNA has gained primary importance in medical research, proving paternity, and in catching criminals.

In 1940, there were 30 million telephones in the US. The home telephones were mostly party lines where several neighbors shared the same telephone line. You could listen in on your neighbor's conversation. Cell phones showed up around 1993. Today, four of every ten people you pass on the street are using their telephone for something. Clerks in stores do not want to help you because they are on their phones...

In the 1940's, automobiles were big and made out of steel. There was no air conditioning. The most expensive ones had radios. There was no independent suspension, no fuel injection, no stereo satellite radio, and no foreign brands. Today, there is all of that and more.

Up to the 1960's, commercial airplanes were the propeller types with slow air speeds. Today they are Dreamliner supersonic jets capable of carrying over 400 passengers flying across the Atlantic in 7–8 hours. When I was born, that trip was usually done by ship and took 7–8 days.

Sexual behavior that used to be immoral, illegal and shamed by society is now protected by law and promoted in all forms of media.

When I first entered the accounting profession, most of the data was accounted for manually. Inventories were taken by going to the warehouse and counting each item. My firm got its first computer in 1970 and it took up a 1,000 sq. ft. room with special air conditioning and ventilation. Today, a laptop processes many times more data at many times more rapid speeds, and inventories are done by the auditor's laptop accessing the client's computer records.

Today, everything is faster and bigger and smaller. And they get faster and bigger and smaller every month.

I could go on with the major changes in my world that have taken place in my life time, but I'm sure you get the idea. All of the changes I have mentioned constitute major paradigm changes in every area of my generation's lives. No other generation has experienced this many life-changing changes. To change from a Galaxy 5 to a Galaxy 6 or an iPhone 5 to an iPhone 6 is not a paradigm change.

I have made many paradigm changes in my life and I am tired. When I left the accounting profession, I was working with an older man, a smart man with a Harvard MBA, who said, "God got this aging thing right. About the time you can't stand to live in the world anymore it is time for you to die." He echoed what Sigmund Freud said six decades earlier, "The gods are merciful when they make our lives more unpleasant as we grow old. In the end death seems less intolerable than the many burdens we have to bear." I am not an old man who as yet finds life unpleasant nor are my burdens too much for me. For the past 25 years my life has been a joy and when my time to die comes will I be ready? Psychologically, I am there.

Next, we will look at death as it is dealt with in the disciplines of literature, philosophy, psychology and theology. Are they a source of contentment as we pass through death's door?

Death in literature

Many an author has taken what Marcus Aurelius wrote about the act of dying being one of the acts of life to heart. From the earliest known literature, the human consciousness of its own mortality has provided subjects for literature. The meaning and nature of life and death as the ultimate existential unknown have been written about extensively in poems, plays, novels and religious scriptures.

John Skelton writing in the journal *BJPsych Advances* published by the Royal College of Psychiatrists says, "One of the central tasks of literature is to impose a structure on life and death, giving meaning to both. Indeed, literature as a discipline aims just as certainly as science does to understand the world in which we live and to interpret our own role as participants in the human condition." To be sure, our last role in the human condition is to die. How we play our part depends a lot on how we lived. If we live what we consider to be a good moral life and yet suffer in dying we feel cheated—where is the justice? If we live a bad life and suffer in dying we think we deserve it. If we lived a bad life and are dying an easy death we wonder—is justice waiting on the other side? I don't deserve an easy death. There are many variations of the death scene in literature and many emotions expressed by those authors who write about death.

One such author wrote the Book of Job in the Bible. Most scholars believe Job lived between 3000–2000 BC. Yet Job's words could have been written today. He says in Chapter 7, "My days are swifter than a weaver's shuttle, and they come to an end without hope." Job is suffering terribly in his middle years and thinks he is suffering unto death. He goes on to say, "I will speak out in the anguish of my spirit, I will complain in the bitterness of my soul." He goes on to say in Chapter 30, "I cry out to you, O God, but you do not answer ... I know you will bring me down to death, to the place appointed for all the living." Later on in Chapter 38 God addresses Job's complaint with simple questions: "Have the gates of death been shown to you? Have you seen the gates of the shadow of death?" Yes, Job had lived a righteous life and, yes, Job was suffering greatly. He was dealing with a theme that has been repeated over and over again in literature—why do the righteous suffer and die just like the unrighteous? The book of Job ends with the words, "And so he died, old and full of years." I encourage you to read the last chapter and see what turned it around for him.

I could mention hundreds of classic works of literature that deal with death. Many of Shakespeare's works center on that theme, *King Lear*, for instance. Edgar Allan Poe's philosophy of death stands out prominently in most of his works. He lived a hard life and died a sudden tragic and pointless death which he had no time to philosophize over. Willa Cather's *A Death in the Desert,* William Faulkner's *As I Lay Dying*, and Emily Dickinson's poem "Death is a Dialogue" are some other examples. I want to deal with two more examples in some greater detail to illustrate how art imitates life with the last act being the act of death.

Death of a Salesman, written by Arthur Miller, has been described as "a play in two acts and a requiem." It was later made into a movie. Miller described it as "the tragedy of a man who gave his life, or sold it" in pursuit of the American Dream. The main character is a travelling salesman named Willy Loman. Willy has spent his adult life selling himself with a "smile and a shoeshine" as he chased the big sales which would provide the income to pay for his "American Dream." He has the house, the appliances, the wife and the two sons that the Dream requires. However, the house and the appliances are encumbered with payments, the wife feels abandoned and hates her husband and the sons are failures in their father's eyes; but not as much a failure as he is in their eyes. Willy eventually loses his job and mooches off his successful neighbor. During all of this, Willy lives a daydream life of success for him and his sons.

The reality is that all their lives are failures according to the American Dream. The older son has a dream of a business proposition that needs $20,000 to get started. His entire career Willy knew that the product he sold was ultimately himself as he sold out to the American Dream. The final sale he made was his own life, which he sold for the life insurance money so that his son could become a "success" in business. Willy Loman led a miserable life and died every way but physically. Then he committed suicide to complete the process. After the poorly attended funeral, the wife begins to sob, repeating "We're free...." Loman had a living death, dying a little every day. In the end, his physical death produced more value than his living death ever did. That is not the kind of old man I want to be or the kind of death I want to die.

Another literary work that attracted my attention was Leo Tolstoy's *The Death of Ivan Ilyich*. This work tells the story of the death, at age 45, of a successful high-court judge in nineteenth-century Russia. Ilyich was living his own version of the American Dream before it ever came to America. He is working his way up the social ladder as he works his way up the professional ladder. It is a story all too familiar today, as Ilyich is enjoying the good life outside the home, his home life is deteriorating. Like Willy Loman, he has a dreadful relationship with his wife and children.

One day he injures his side while hanging curtains in a new apartment that reflects his superior status in society. The injury is not correctly diagnosed and it becomes clear to all that Ilyich is dying. The meat of the story is how Ilyich wrestles with the idea of his own immortality. While his pain is growing worse and worse he wonders, "How can this be?" In his own mind he has lived rightly and does not deserve to suffer. He could understand suffering in death if he had not lived a good life. Therefore, suffering and death must be arbitrary and senseless.

Making it even more difficult for Ilyich to accept his imminent death is the fact that his wife, children, doctor and friends will not talk to him about his death. They only acknowledge to him that he is sick and not dying. That only denies him the comfort of other people as he lies dying. Then he begins to hate them. The only person in his life who seems to understand what he is going through and who comforts him is his servant boy.

In his final days, Ilyich begins to question whether he has, in fact, lived a good life. He looks back over his life and sees how artificial it was. He looks at his servant boy's life and sees how authentic it is. The artificial life is a self-centered life. The authentic life is a life of compassion and sympathy for others. He then realizes his was not a good, authentic life. He ends up pitying his wife and children for having to put up with his artificial life and hopes his death will release them. With this change of heart, the pain and terror of death leave him. Is it too late to make things right? In his dying moments, with his family around him Tolstoy writes, "He tried to say 'forgive', but said 'forgo'…and too weak to correct himself, shook his [son's] hand, knowing that he [God] would understand whose understanding mattered." Then in place of death there was light and he exclaimed, "What joy!" Then, "Death is over. It's no more."

This work was written after Tolstoy had his religious conversion around 1880 and attracted my attention because it is basically my personal story. I lived the kind of artificial, self-centered life that Ivan Ilyich lived up until the time of my Christian conversion. I went through the same process of seeking forgiveness from those whom I had hurt that Ilyich did. My old self died and a new self came to life, an authentic life of compassion and sympathy for others. The only difference is my physical death is still in the future but, for me, the fear of that death is gone.

I write all this to say that literature can help you learn about death through somebody else's experience, whether fiction or real. Many of you are living or have lived the Willy Loman and the Ivan Ilyich kind of life. Would you be more valuable to your family after you are dead than you are while you are alive? Will you see the truth of the emptiness of the artificial self-centered life before death is knocking on your door? If you are converted now, death will lose its sting.

Maybe literature is not your thing. Philosophy has had a lot to say on the subject of death for many centuries. Is there any light in philosophy?

Death in philosophy

I want to be the kind of old man who is philosophically prepared for death. The subject of death is alive and well in the discipline of philosophy. In fact, it has been assigned its own "philosophy of" division in philosophical studies. Many university philosophy departments offer courses on the Philosophy of Death. *The Oxford Handbook of Philosophy of Death* was published in 2012. The International Association for the Philosophy of Death and Dying (IAPDD) is a global organization that held its inaugural conference in 2014. I am not going to give you an exhaustive treatise on philosophy and death, but just enough to let you know that, for centuries and centuries, much has been said and written by philosophers about death but nothing has been done about it. It is kind of like the weather in that respect and kind of like science in that philosophy never has a last word. Philosophy comes from the human mind and until the last human has lost his mind there will be philosophy.

On a side note before I go on, one of the things I have observed as I have researched for this section is that some authors are not always careful as to who they attribute philosophical quotes to. That is caused somewhat by philosophers' propensity to paraphrase what earlier philosophers have said. As Cicero has said, "There is nothing so absurd that some philosopher has not already said it."

According to Cicero, as paraphrased by Montaigne, "To philosophize is to learn how to die." Death is a fact of life. You can't live with it and you can't live without it. In other words, it is a fertile field for philosophizing. Of course, one's view of death hinges on one's view of what happens to you when you die. The great Socrates had his suspicions but he also had his doubts. He said:

> *To fear death, my friends, is only to think ourselves wise, without being wise: for it is to think that we know what we do not know. For anything that man can tell, death may be the greatest good that can happen to them; but they fear it as if they knew quite well that it was the greatest of evils. And what is this but that shameful ignorance of thinking that we know what we do not know?*

That shameful ignorance has not stopped philosophers from philosophizing about death for the past 2,500 years.

The Stoic philosopher Seneca wrote, "He will live badly who does not know how to die well." He was ordered by Nero to commit suicide, which he did, but did not do it very well. First, the cutting of arteries to bleed to death, but he bled too slowly to die, so he took poison which did not kill him. Finally, he was taken into a steam bath and was suffocated by the steam ... now I forget why I'm telling you this!

Living badly, dying well; living well, dying badly; living badly, dying badly; or living well, dying well (I think those are all the options) are all dependent upon what happens at and after death. Every philosophy of life has a philosophy of the afterlife, or it doesn't. And the two are tied together. Here's what I mean.

Every philosopher has/had a philosophy of life that of necessity included a philosophy of death because no philosopher believed they would live in their body forever. Some feared death; some helped it along. The philosopher Albert Camus wrote, "There is one truly serious philosophical problem, and that is suicide." I printed out a list from the Internet that showed how notable philosophers died. The list had 78 names of notable philosophers showing that 30% of them committed suicide. The suicide rate in the US is .0125% and in the UK is .0118%. If the one truly serious philosophical problem is suicide, the problem seems to be the philosophers themselves. Or maybe they did not understand the seriousness of the problem.

Death, you see, poses its own question. The question is "Then what?" For those philosophers that believe death of the body is the cessation of existence of that person in any form, the "then" part of the question does not apply because there is no "then" for a person to exist in. "Then" is a period of time that comes after a previous period of time. For those philosophers that believe there is an afterlife of some form, the "what" part of the question kicks in. We will look at what a few of the notable philosophers had to say about the "then" and the "what" of death.

First, some basics. When it comes to the nature of us human beings, philosophy is divided into two camps. The materialists believe that physical matter is the only or fundamental reality and that all being, processes, and phenomena can be explained as manifestations of matter in some form. This camp believes that no mind, soul or spirit exists in a person. What is perceived to be those things are only functions of cells in the brain. The other camp is called the dualists who believe that human beings are constituted of material and immaterial elements or matter and spirit. They recognize the possibility that the immaterial part of people may continue to exist after the death of the material part (the body). What camp the philosopher belongs to will determine their answer to the "what" part of the question.

Another basic philosophical understanding of "what" after death is the difference between afterlife and immortality. Some philosophers believe in an afterlife but not immortality. Afterlife is the continuation of a person's existence after death regardless of whether or not that continuation is indefinite. In other words, the immaterial elements of a person could continue to exist a short time after death and then fade away. Immortality implies a never-ending existence.

"To be or not to be, that is the question." Socrates has allowed for both possibilities in his philosophy of death or maybe we should call it "death doubt." He appears to have believed that the human soul existed before physical birth because a person seems to know things innately that they have not been taught in this life. But what happens after death, he was not sure. On his death bed he said, "The hour of departure has arrived and we go our ways; I to die, and you to live. Which is better? Only God knows." (It is hard to know what god Socrates believed in. He was accused by the State of not believing in the Greek gods.) He said that death brought one of two possibilities: "Either it is annihilation, and the dead have no consciousness of anything; or, as we are told, it is really a change: a migration of the soul from this place to another." With a beginning like that, no wonder philosophy is still seeking wisdom. He went on to say that it did not matter which of these possibilities was true and that death was not something to be feared. He believed that if the soul continued to exist it would be a pleasant existence with old friends and Greek heroes who have died.

On the other hand, the ancient Greek philosopher, Epicurus, who has a school of philosophy named after him, took a stand on the annihilation, or cease to exist, side. He wrote, "To practice living well and to practice dying well are one and the same." He went on to say, "Death is nothing to us, since when we are, death has not come, and when death has come, we are not." Maybe his head is out of the sand now.

This could go on and on but I am going to skip to the twentieth-century German philosopher, Martin Heidegger (1889–1976), because his views on death and "then what" have the greatest influence on the philosophers of today. Heidegger belonged to the Existentialism school of philosophy, which focused on individual existence in an unfathomable universe. They believe that an individual simply exists and has the responsibility to create their own essences by assuming ultimate responsibility for acts of free will without any certain knowledge of what is right or wrong, good or bad. In Heidegger's best known work, *Being and Time*, he posits that being is time. Being is temporal and exists in time between birth and death. Being is time and time is finite for us; it ends at our death. He says that an authentic human being lives with death in mind ("being-towards-death") but for him this was not a dreadful thing. For him, living with awareness of mortality added a zest to life. If we thought we were going to exist forever, life would become dull and routine. It's like knowing you are going to die someday ought to make you enjoy life more. You know, *carpe vita*. And since life is lived one day at a time—*carpe diem*. (Remember, this is a great philosopher speaking.) Needless to say, for this Existentialist, when time stops, being stops, death is the end of existence. Maybe he knows different now.

I'll close this section with some miscellaneous quotes and an observation:

"They tell us that suicide is the greatest piece of cowardice ... that suicide is wrong; when it is quite obvious that there is nothing in the world to which every man has a more unassailable title than to his own life and person."
—Arthur Schopenhauer

"The day which we fear as our last is the birthday of eternity."
—Lucius Annaeus Seneca

"I intend to live forever, or die trying."
—Groucho Marx (How did he get in here?)

"It is possible to provide security against other ills, but as far as death is concerned, we men live in a city without walls."
—Epicurus

"f I take death into my life, acknowledge it, and face it squarely, I will free myself from the anxiety of death and the pettiness of life—and only then will I be free to become myself."
—Martin Heidegger

"Death is not an event in life: we do not live to experience death. If we take eternity to mean not infinite temporal duration but

timelessness, then eternal life belongs to those who live in the present."
—Ludwig Wittgenstein

"I don't believe in an afterlife, although I am bringing a change of underwear."
—Woody Allen (I know how he got in here.)

"Death is not extinguishing the light; it is putting out the lamp because dawn has come."
—Seneca

It is interesting that not many philosophers who believe in some kind of afterlife have produced any ideas on judgment after death. Most, like Socrates, assume that any existence after death will be a good one or it would not exist. Obviously, there is no empirical evidence proving that there is an afterlife or immortality. Whatever the philosopher believes, he believes by faith. It seems to me that faith and afterlife is in the purview of religion. Like scientists, philosophers do not like to acknowledge the role of faith in their beliefs. The German philosopher Friedrich Nietzsche sums up the prevailing attitude with this definition: "Faith: not wanting to know what is true."

Oh well, now we will move on to see if psychology can shed any more light on death.

Death in psychology

I want to be the kind of old man who is psychologically prepared for death. In the area of Human Sciences, psychology as a separate discipline is the new kid on the block. Back around 387 BC, Plato suggested that the brain is the mechanism of mental processes. A few years later Aristotle suggested that the heart is the mechanism of mental processes. That kind of got the ball rolling so that mental processes and the associated emotional states became areas of philosophical investigation. It remained a branch of philosophy for centuries until the 1870's. In the last three decades of the 1800's, formal laboratories of psychology were established in Germany and the United States and psychology developed as an independent scientific discipline. The American Psychological Association was founded in 1892.

Very early in its history, psychological studies were divided between those psychologists who wanted to study behavior from an experimental, physiological perspective and those who wanted to focus on a broader person-based approach. The philosophical theory of logical positivism won the day. Logical positivism is a method of inquiry that requires verifiable consequences in experience as proof of knowledge. It being the case that experience became an area of psychological investigation' it is no wonder that death was not an area of psychological investigation. Who would want to volunteer for this kind of research and voluntarily experience death?

After 50 years of man's inhumanity to man resulting in two World Wars, the area of psychological investigation turned to the person-based approach thinking we better find out what makes people tick. Since death is something every person faces, death became an area of study. Psychology's first organized approach to death was a symposium presented at the 1956 meeting of the American Psychological Association titled, "The Concept of Death and its Relationship to Behavior." It eventually gave rise to the field of "thanatology," which is the study of death, dying, and bereavement. The Thanatology Association currently publishes a professional journal titled *Death Studies*.

There is also a research journal being published titled, *Omega: The Journal of Death and Dying*. Psychology of Death and Dying is in the curriculum of most psychology degrees in most universities. Yes, death is alive and well in the discipline of psychology. So what does psychology have to say about it?

The 1969 book *On Death and Dying* by Elisabeth Kubler-Ross was based on her work with terminally ill patients. The book identifies a series of emotional stages experienced by people dealing with the death of a loved one or their own imminent death. The stages are denial, anger, bargaining, depression, and acceptance. The author placed much emphasis on communication with the person dealing with death. She believed that people want to talk about their life, their particular illness, and their imminent death. Therapy seems to be the psychological way to help people cope with death.

Over the years many studies have been published by psychologists on death attitudes. Four themes have emerged:

- Most people think about death, report some fear of death, but a small minority are preoccupied with their own death.
- More women report fear of death than men.
- The majority of people did not experience an increase of fear of death as their age increased.
- When it comes to their own death, people are more concerned with suffering pain and helplessness and the well-being of loved ones left behind than with their death.

Fear of death and the anxiety it causes still drives psychology's involvement with the process of death.

However, in recent decades dealing with death anxiety as the emphasis of psychology has been joined by the existential quest for death acceptance. New theories have emerged and new models for coping with death have been proposed. For an article in a 2011 issue of *Death Studies*, psychology professors Paul Wong and Adrian Tomer gave this title: "Beyond Terror and Denial: The Positive Psychology of Death Acceptance." They began the article like this: "Death remains the biggest threat as well as the greatest challenge to humanity." (Remember I told you at the beginning of this chapter that more people die of death than any other cause. It is indeed a threat to humanity.) They point out that in the post-9/11, era terrorist attacks are an ever-present threat. So are cancer, automobile accidents, plane crashes, the threat of being killed in a home break-in. With 24-hour TV news coverage of these things, along with natural disasters and wars in other parts of the world, death has invaded our living rooms and is almost constantly before our eyes. It has become a form of entertainment in video games, movies and TV dramas. Their premise is that people's relationship with death needs to move beyond terror and denial toward a more positive attitude toward death. (Now, I have to admit right here that there are a few people whose death I have a positive attitude toward, but that is not what they mean.) They are talking about moving beyond the fear of death because that fear "can prevent us from living fully and vitally because so much energy will be spent in the denial and avoidance of death."

Wong and his associates Reher and Gesser have developed the Death Attitude Profile (DAP) and identified three distinct types of death acceptance: (a) *neutral death acceptance* in which the person faces death rationally as the inevitable end of life; (b) *approach acceptance* in which the person sees death as the gateway to a better afterlife; and, (c) *escape acceptance* in which the person accepts death as a better alternative to a painful existence. This has given rise to other psychologists developing what they call terror management theory (TMT). TMT posits that the "avoidance of death anxiety is the primary motive while the quest for positive meaning is secondary, because the latter is used as a way to shield us from the terror of death."

For every action there is an equal and opposite reaction, right? TMT gave rise to meaning management theory (MMT) in which the quest for meaning is the primary motive for treatment. According to MMT, the quest for meaning in life enables us to live fully in the light of death. Then there is self-determination theory (SDT) which emphasizes that "healthy people seek authentic meaning as opposed to the defensive or contingent self-esteem emphasized in TMT." I don't know, but it seems to me that healthy people would not be bothered with anxiety about their death or meaning to their existence. People worried about those things tend to not be healthy.

Wong and Tomer go on to say that in order to achieve a complete psychology of death there needs to be some interrelation between defense-oriented theories, such as TMT, and growth-oriented models, like MMT and SDT, that emphasize meaning seeking and meaning making as a basic human motivation. It seems that where psychology of death is now is more existential. Regarding death as a reminder of our own mortality and the need to live authentic lives can cause death anxiety to facilitate death acceptance and encourage us on to self-actualization.

I found a quote by a rock guitarist who was told he had cancer and only 8–9 months to live. He was seeing everything from a different perspective and said, "Wow, why didn't I work this out before? Why didn't I work out before that it's just the moment you're in that matters?" He had bought in to MMT and

SDT. Facing up to the reality of death greatly reduces the associated anxiety of death.

Maybe you have noticed some familiar terms in this section on psychology that we used in the section on philosophy. "Existential," "authentic life," "created meaning," these are all associated with the philosophy of existentialism. Remember Heidegger's concept of "being towards death"? In how it deals with death, it seems that in its relationship with philosophy, psychology has moved out but it has not moved on. They both leave us at *carpe diem*, but without contentment.

Death in religion

I want to be the kind of old man who is spiritually prepared for death. As we have seen, philosophy and psychology try to help you deal with living in the specter of death, but they do not have answers for the "Then what?" question.

In football terminology, when it comes to the forth down of life and you either go for it or punt, philosophy and psychology punt and give the ball to religion, which they bet against. Philosopher George Santayana wrote, "Each religion, by the help of more or less myth, which it takes more or less seriously, proposes some method of fortifying the human soul and enabling it to make its peace with its destiny." Psychologist Sigmund Freud said, "Religion is an illusion and it derives its strength from the fact that it falls in with our instinctual desires." He did get the last two words right. Eternity is an instinctual desire in human beings and it is God-given. The book of Ecclesiastes (3:11) says that God has set eternity in the hearts of man. That is the reason man believes in life after death and looks to religion to reveal the afterlife. Philosophy and psychology cannot do it. Religions, with few exceptions, answer the "then" part of the question with an affirmation of an afterlife that is continued existence after physical death. The "what" part of the question has almost as many answers as there are religions in the world. We will only take the time to deal with the major ones.

Religions give guidance for both sides of the great divide. They give instructions in the form of teachings or commandments for living before you die which, if followed in life, will affect the "Then what?" aspect of death. If a person is trusting the physical life to a religion, they are automatically putting their afterlife into the same hands. The law of logic called the Law of Non-contradiction goes back to Aristotle and says that, "opposite assertions cannot both be true at the same time." The reason Islam is not Hinduism is because they make conflicting assertions about how to live life and what happens after death. The same can be said about any two religions and all religions in general. They all make assertions that differ from the assertions made by all other religions. You know what that means, folks—only one religion can assert what is true compared with all the rest. That means you better be careful what hands you trust your afterlife to because all but one have holes in them.

My purpose in this section is not to give an exhaustive presentation of the beliefs of various religions on life, death and afterlife. Don't fault me if I leave something out because I am leaving almost everything out. Please do your own investigation, because the consequences of what you choose to believe are eternal whether you choose to believe that or not. That is my disclaimer! Within most major world religions there are sects that alter the assertions of that religion somewhat and in the West, some popular cults have spun off of Christianity, but I will not deal with the sects and cults. To refresh your memory we will take a brief tour of what is on offer in these world religions.

Starting in the East, the Chinese religion of Taoism and Confucianism are not true religions, but philosophies of life or systems of ethics. Religious factors were added later. Tao means "the Way" of ultimate reality by which one should order one's life. They believe a life energy flows throughout the human body and the universe unifying everything. There is no belief in a personal deity and they seek to live by the "three jewels" of compassion, moderation, and humility. Taoists are not concerned with eternity but only with living the right kind of life on a daily basis separated from worldly or social concerns. That is its own reward.

On the other hand, Confucianism teaches that people can live a good life only in a well-disciplined society that stresses attention to ceremony, duty, morality, and public service. The goal of Confucianism is *Chun-tan*, the perfect human being; mature, self-controlled, helpful to others. There are no deities or teachings about an afterlife in Confucianism. It is a philosophy of life that functions as a religion to teach people how to live. When Buddhism arrived in China in the first century AD, its teachings on an afterlife influenced Taoism and Confucianism and added a religious dimension to these philosophies.

Buddhism was founded around 500 BC by the Buddha, Siddhartha Gautama. He left no writings and many centuries passed before some of his teachings were written down. Buddhism is also a philosophy for living pursuing the Middle Way by avoiding extreme asceticism and extreme luxury. The goal is enlightenment, which is variously defined as a state in which the individual transcends desire and suffering and attains Nirvana (nothingness, cessation of everything). Enlightenment is the wisdom that comes from the direct experience of all phenomena being empty of independent existence. To help you get there, Buddhism offers the Eight-fold Path of right views; right thought; right speech; right conduct; right livelihood; right effort; right mindfulness; and, right concentration. Buddha himself is the only one believed to have reached Enlightenment.

Hinduism also has Nirvana as its goal but it is a different Nirvana from Buddhism. Hinduism sees life as a cycle of reincarnations into a higher or lower caste based on one's Karma (actions or consequences thereof) in life. Nirvana in Hinduism is not nothingness as in Buddhism, but everythingness. Brahman is the consciousness of the universe seen as the ultimate deity. Enlightenment is attained by becoming tuned in to the Brahman within. Atman (the self-consciousness, the divine soul in every creature) is Brahman is the goal. That is salvation and can be achieved in one of four ways: the Way of Works; the Way of Knowledge; the Way of Devotion; and, the Way of Yoga. There is a pantheon of gods available to help you on the way to everythingness.

When it comes to the major world religions, the new kid on the block is Islam. Islam was started in Saudi Arabia by an Arab named Mohammed around 600 AD. He claimed to have had a series of visions over 23 years which are recorded in what became the Koran. The bottom line of his visions was "There is no God but Allah. Life must be lived in complete submission to the will of Allah." Mohammed could neither read nor write so he repeated his visions to his followers who memorized them and committed them to writing after Mohammed died. The content of the Koran shows Jewish and Christian influence. To be a Muslim (practitioner of Islam), you must submit to five obligations (the "Five Pillars"). You must profess, "There is no God but Allah, and Mohammed is his messenger"; pray five times a day; fast during the month of Ramadan; give alms to the poor; and make a pilgrimage to Mecca if physically and financially able. After death, one will reside in the grave until the appointed day of resurrection and judgment. Salvation is earned by believing and keeping the tenets of Islam but is not guaranteed. Only those who give their lives for the cause of Islam are guaranteed Paradise. According to Muslim belief, everything one longs for in this life will be there in Paradise for him. Of course, Allah will be there, but the emphasis is on physical and sensual pleasures.

Judaism, on the other hand, has no definitive teaching about an afterlife. Its most important religious text, the Torah, is silent on the subject. Over the centuries, several teachings have developed, but none is definitive for all Judaism. The teachings center around *olam ha-ba*, which literally means, "the world to come" in Hebrew. It is a physical realm that will exist after the Jewish Messiah comes and the dead are resurrected and judged. Until that time, some believe that the souls of those who die in a righteous state will go to a place like the Garden of Eden to await the resurrection, while the souls of those who die in an unrighteous state go to Gehenna, a place of punishment. Beliefs vary as to what happens to the soul after the resurrection, from the unrighteous being annihilated to them spending eternity in hell. Most that believe in a resurrection believe the righteous will spend eternity in a Garden of Eden kind of place.

Christianity has a complete eschatology extending to the final eternal state of the world, so, obviously, it answers the "Then what?" question. In Christianity, the key to the "what" part is the person's relationship with God when he dies. Christ is the key in Christianity and faith in him is the key to a right relationship with God. Those who die "in Christ," that is, having faith in his death on the cross as payment for our sin-debt to God will have their spirits (souls) ushered into the presence of Christ to await the resurrection of the bodies. The spirits of those who die not believing in Christ will be sent to Hades until the resurrection and final judgment when they will spend eternity in Hell. A minority of Christians believes the souls of the believers and unbelievers will sleep, or be in an unconscious state, until the resurrection and final judgment.

There is a common misconception among non-Christians that Christianity has a list of Commandments from Moses and Jesus that must be obeyed if a person is to go to Heaven. Unlike other religions, where the place of final destiny is determined by what you do (works) to earn a pleasant afterlife, in Christianity the place of the afterlife is determined solely upon whether one believes in Jesus Christ as his Lord and Savior. When a person is truly a Christian through faith in Christ, he is changed on the inside to where he wants to obey the commandments and teachings of Christ out of gratitude and love; not because he has to in order to earn Heaven, but because he wants to. That is one big difference between Christianity and all other of the world's religions. In Christianity, a good afterlife (heaven) is a gift of God's grace to those who have faith in His Son, Jesus Christ, to save them. There is nothing a person can do to earn it.

It is impossible for someone writing about a particular religion to really capture the essence of that religion unless he is an adherent, believer and practitioner of that religion. In my effort to write about religions I have not tried to capture the essence of any, but only to briefly describe what the religion teaches about an existence after death. I have studied world religions, having a PhD in Religious Studies, but that only magnifies my mistakes. If I have misrepresented the afterlife in any religion, it was not intentional. In trusting one's soul to a belief system about the afterlife it is important to get it right.

Since I am doing the writing, I am going to take the opportunity to briefly explain why I am a Christian. I was raised by Christian parents and was trained in Christian doctrine as a child. However, that did not make me a Christian any more than knowing that aspirin helps a headache makes me a doctor. When I was old enough to leave home, I left the church and for 20 years lived as if there was no God but me. Then there came a time when I was in the pit of despair and saw no way out. One day I was sitting on a seawall in Florida hopeless and helpless and wanting to die. In that moment I cried out to Jesus to help me and in that moment he did.

Now, here is why from that moment I have been a real Christian and not just an adherent to Christianity. Remember, in our discussion of philosophy and death, the Existential philosophers sought an authentic life based on actual experience. Well, in that moment I became an Existentialist. I had an actual experience that changed my existence. At that moment I became a new and different person. I saw everything differently from before. All my anger was gone. Instead of hatred I felt sorry for the people who had hurt me. More importantly, I felt sorry for the people I had hurt and I felt great remorse for doing so. Remember I told you earlier that I did not want to be an old man with regrets, so, I found as many victims as I could and apologized to them. I changed and my life changed from that moment on the seawall.

After that experience I began investigating the truth claims of Christianity to see what really caused my life to change so dramatically so quickly. What we know about Christ and Christianity we learn from the Bible. Can the Bible be trusted? Is it really the Word of God written by men of God inspired by the Spirit of God? If so, it is different from all other religious texts. Others may claim it, but where is the proof? That led me to study Christian Apologetics, where the evidences supporting the truth claims of Christianity are presented. There I found out that the Bible was written by 40 independent authors during a

1,500 year time span and, yet, it is one continuous story that reads like the work of one author. The clincher for me is the inclusion of prophecies. No other book records prophecies relating to people, nations and events in great detail written hundreds of years in advance and those prophecies being fulfilled exactly as recorded. Only an all-knowing God could inspire that.

No other religion has a founder who walked the earth claiming to be God and performing miracles, signs and wonders to prove it. No other founder of a religion, except Jesus Christ, taught that there would be a resurrection of the dead and rose from the dead himself to prove it. The resurrection of Jesus Christ is attested to by eyewitnesses who saw him after he rose from the dead and by non-Christian historians of the time. I won't go any farther. I just wanted you to know why I believe Christianity to be the truth and the worldview it holds is one that is liveable and accords with reality. The evidence is there for anyone who cares to investigate. But the only proof I need is the metaphysical change in me.

Well, I hope you are not bored to death with reading about death. Actually, I hope you are still reading. I don't want to be the kind of old man who goes on for pages and chapters, but this is an important subject, especially to old people. And religion is the only discipline that purports to deal with the "Then what?" question. In the words of the Apostle Paul, "If only for this life we have hope in Christ, we are to be pitied more than all men. But Christ has indeed been raised from the dead."

> "We can believe what we choose.
> We are answerable for what we choose to believe."
> —Cardinal John Henry Newman

[7]

Life: The Meaning of the Story

> "Socrates said that the unexamined life is not worth living—But what if the examined life turns out to be a clunker as well?"
> —Kurt Vonnegut

I CERTAINLY WANT TO BE the kind of old man who can say that the story of my life has meaning. Of course, this raises the much debated question, "What is the meaning of life?" To make sure we are all on the same page, we need to define the terms. By "life" do we mean the universal or the particulars? Do we mean human life in general on planet earth or do we mean every particular individual's life? And what does "meaning" mean? Does it mean finding a purpose and fulfilling that purpose? Does it have to do with value, worth or significance? Now, I am writing like a true philosopher: I am asking questions but not giving answers. Here is one answer. By "life" I am talking about each individual life; a person lives, a person dies—did his life have meaning? The meaning of "meaning" has generated much discussion in the various fields of human sciences that we have heard from before. I'll give a brief overview of what they say on the subject of the meaning of life and then I will give you what can reasonably be the right answer.

Literature has many words but not many answers as to the meaning of life. Beginning with Homer's *Iliad*, written around 800 BC, which depicted Achilles in the position of having to choose to go into battle or not. To not go would lead to a long life, but a life of shame. To go into battle would mean that he would die young, but dying in battle would bring honor and glory. What meaning did he want for his life? Later authors such as Sophocles, Euripides and Dante examined human life from the standpoint of the gods, or God, giving meaning to it. William Shakespeare was one of the first literary figures to use human experience as the grounds upon which meaning of life may be speculated. This is what he wrote in *Macbeth*:

Life's but a walking shadow, a poor player

That struts and frets his hour upon the stage

And then is heard no more. It is a tale

Told by an idiot, full of sound and fury

Signifying nothing.

—Macbeth (Act 5, Scene 5, lines 17–28)

In 1896, German author Thomas Mann wrote a story called *Disillusionment*. It is the story of two strangers that end up sitting close to each other in a piazza in Venice. One does all the talking. He asked the other (the storyteller) if Venice came up to his expectations and then asked the telling question, "You did not picture it as finer than the reality?" This was his first hint of disillusionment. Then he asked the storyteller, "Do you know, my dear sir, what disillusionment is?" He began to relate how all of life has been a great disappointment and disillusionment for him. When he was a child, his home caught on fire and was completely destroyed. Afterwards he thought, "This is what it is like to have the house on fire. Is this all there is to it?"

Later on in life he stood in front of great works of art and said to himself: "It is beautiful, and yet—is that all? Is it no more beautiful than that?" Then he fell in love with a girl that loved and married somebody else and he thought: "So this is the greatest pain we can suffer. Well, and what then—is this all?" When he saw the sea for the first time he was excited because it was big and he longed to be free. But then he saw the horizon. "Why a horizon, when I wanted the infinite from life?" Then he waited for death and said that at his last moment he would be saying to himself: "So this is the great experience—well, and what of it? What is it after all?" Unfortunately, this man's story is a lot of people's story.

I was in college in the 1960's, the decade when Western society made a sharp turn to the left and threw off the shackles of tradition and morality. At the end of that decade Peggy Lee recorded a hit song titled, "Is That all there Is?" It was written by Leiber and Stoller, who were inspired to write it by that Thomas Mann story. The lyrics come straight from the story. Each verse tells of an incident in life that left the singer disillusioned and after each verse there is the refrain. The first verse is about the child's house fire and the question, "Is that all there is to the fire?" The second verse is about a trip to the circus and the question, "Is that all there is to a circus?" And then the falling in love and the question "Is that all there is to love?" The last verse asked why the singer does not end it all, but that would only bring the final disappointment and the question, "Is that all there is?" The refrain after each verse captures the angst of the age:

> Is that all there is?
> Is that all there is?
> If that is all there is my friends,
> Then let's keep dancing.
> Let's break out the booze and have a ball,
> If that's all there is.

This song was recorded again for this generation by Bette Midler in 2005. The sentiments of the lyrics are expressed in much of the rap and rock music of today. There is a general feeling of disillusionment and that one's life has no meaning. But that does not have to be the case.

We have looked in some detail at Willie Loman in Arthur Miller's *Death of a Salesman* and Tolstoy's *The Death of Ivan Illyich* and their search for meaning in their lives. When it comes right down to it, all an author can do is create a life and then hold it up to the light and examine it. He is like a scientist who can only examine microbes under a microscope and describe what he sees as biological life. To ascribe any meaning to what he sees, like the writer, he must appeal to information he receives from other sources. In other words, to describe the life of a character with all its emotions, successes and failures does not give meaning to that life. The search for the meaning of life must move outside literature.

Not many philosophy dictionaries have an entry for "meaning of life," but the First Edition of *The Oxford Dictionary of Philosophy* does. It begins by stating, "For nearly everyone it is important to think that his or her life has a purpose. But these purposes may be various: the purpose of one's life may be to achieve one kind of goal, that of another person may be to achieve a very different kind of goal. There need be no one thing that forms the purpose of every life." Take note of the "purpose" and "achieve one kind of goal" as it is attributed to the meaning of life. Plato said the meaning of life is achieving the goal of attaining the highest form of knowledge, which in his view is the Ideal or Form of the Good, from which all good and just things derive utility and value. Aristotle said that knowing the Good was not good enough—you have to achieve the goal of being good and virtuous. And that means happiness, well-being and excellence in successful living. Now, that is a good promise, but is it true?

Later philosophers have limited the goal to happiness alone; a happy life is a meaningful life. The Epicureans taught the source of happiness to be modest pleasures, freedom from fear and bodily pain, and limiting one's desires for the things of this world (sounds like Buddhism), thus having a trouble-free soul that dies when the body dies. This meaningful life can be attained by sober reasoning and right beliefs. The Stoics took it a step further. Their road to happiness was one of the use of reason to develop personal self-control as the means of overcoming destructive emotions and desires.

Around the turn of the nineteenth century, Jeremy Bentham founded the school of thought called Utilitarianism. He defined the meaning of life as the "greatest happiness principle," which says that "the good is whatever brings the greatest happiness to the greatest number of people." So making other people happy (and lots of them) will give my life meaning. The position of the philosophical school of Nihilism holds that life is without objective meaning. Pragmatism says the meaning of life is discoverable only by way of experience. In other words, when you have it, then you will know what it is. Existentialism says that each human being creates the essence, or meaning, of his or her life. To do that, we must use more than reason (because it gives rise to emotions of anxiety, dread, and the awareness of dread), moving on to a commitment to one's own values and goals in an aimless and irrational world. That commitment brings meaning.

Getting us up to date, Postmodern philosophy has this to say: "Anything resembling a 'meaning of life', in postmodern terms, can only be understood within a social and linguistic framework, and must be pursued as an escape from power structures that are already embedded in all forms of speech and interaction." I acknowledge that I have given very simplistic short summaries of what some schools of philosophy say about the meaning of life. However, if you were to read everything the philosophers wrote, I don't think you would come to any different conclusions or inconclusions on what they offer.

All of the historical philosophical views on the meaning of life can be captured in four views that dominate today and they can be divided into the two broad headings of naturalism and supernaturalism. Under naturalism you have objective naturalism, which holds that a meaningful life is possible without a supernatural realm since there is not one. For them, a meaningful life is a function of making a mind-independent connection with something inherently valuable, but you could be wrong about what you consider to be inherently valuable. Subjective naturalism says that what constitutes a meaningful life is a function of getting what you want and achieving goals you set for yourself. Of course, that means the definition of a meaningful life varies from person to person. Pessimistic naturalism is nihilism and denies that a meaningful life is possible because nothing has any value. A nihilist can believe that a connection to a supernatural realm is necessary for a meaningful life, but he also believes that a supernatural realm does not exist so a meaningful life is impossible.

Supernaturalism posits that God exists and that a right relationship with God is the only sufficient way to have a meaningful life. Naturally, the supernatural view is held by very few philosophers, with the majority preferring to shuffle it off to theology. The search for the meaning of life must move beyond philosophy.

Psychology has historically been remiss in addressing the meaning of one's life as it relates to psychological well-being. It is only in the past few years that any research in the area has been done, but even that is sparse. George Kleftaras and Evangelia Psarra did a 2012 study in Greece titled "Meaning in Life, Psychological Well-Being and Depressive Symptomatology: A Comparative Study," published in the journal *Psychology*. They found that subjects with a higher level of life meaning exhibited lower depressive symptomatology and were in better psychological health. Surprise, surprise! Their conclusion was that more studies need to be done in this area.

The field of positive psychology studies "empirical factors that lead to life satisfaction; full engagement in activities makes a fuller contribution by utilizing one's personal strengths, and meaning based on investing in something larger than self." For them meaning of life and fulfillment come with mastering challenging tasks which brings positive feelings. But the task itself might be meaningless. Shades of objective naturalism.

A new kid on the psychological block is natural psychology. A course overview linked on the naturalpsychology.net website states: "You can't find the meaning of life—it never was lost! Meaning never was something to be found in a philosophy, a religion, a belief system, or a way of life. Rather, meaning is a psychological experience. And because it is a psychological experience, you can create it." It goes on to say, "Natural psychology, the first psychology of meaning, spells out how you can fill your life with meaning by creating it." So, if everybody can create their own meaning of life it is subjective and varies from person to person. Shades of subjective naturalism.

It seems to me that what we have encountered in this human science is philosophy with a psychology degree. The search for the meaning of life must move beyond psychology.

The search for the meaning of life should end with theology. But before we go there I want to give you a sample of people's thinking today about this all-important question: "What is the meaning of life?" The magazine *Philosophy Now* asked the question of readers and posted some of their responses in the Feb/Mar 2015 issue:

- I am not convinced there is one right way to live. To suggest that there is demonstrates not so much arrogance as a lack of imagination.
- Surely the goal of meaning of human life is therefore none other than finding oneself becoming a mature adult free to make one's own decisions, yet wanting everyone in the world to have the same advantage.
- Life is existence: it seems "good" to be part of life. But really that's your lot. ... Our over-evolved human minds want more, but unfortunately there is nothing more.
- To "find meaning in life" is a better way of approaching the issue, i.e., whilst there is no single meaning of life, every person can live their life in a way which brings them as much fulfillment and contentment as possible.
- Therefore, liberty is the meaning of life.
- The meaning of life is not being dead.

This sample is representative of the current thinking (or lack thereof) on the meaning of life in this generation.

You might note that all the responses pertained to this life only and none included the idea of purpose. To me, meaning and purpose are the two legs to the two-legged human life. Surely Theology will link these two legs into a meaningful human life.

I do not find help in the Eastern religions. In Taoism, the meaning of life is to realize the temporal nature of existence. The goal is to rejoin the Oneness of the universe by way of self-realization.

Confucianism teaches that a person can realize the ultimate meaning of life in ordinary human existence. It is here that virtue can be achieved through strong relationships and reasoning and minimizing the negative aspects of life.

In Hinduism, the meaning of life is found in the concept of karma and the cycle of birth and rebirth. The goal is liberation from this cycle and the burden of karma, resulting in the union of the soul with the universe.

Buddhism does not teach that life has a meaning or a purpose. Human life has the potential to eliminate suffering. The goal is Nirvana, meaning freedom from suffering and rebirth in a state of nothingness. (Remember the thus-ness of nothingness from the last chapter? You thought I made that up didn't you?)

It has been my experience in talking to adherents and the result of my studies that the adherents of these religions have no testimony of reaching the goal of their religion, but only of striving to reach the targeted goal of meaning. Perhaps the monotheistic religions can help.

In Judaism, the meaning of life is to prepare this physical world for the Messianic era in the future. This can be accomplished through spiritualizing actions in the world between man and his fellowman, and between man and God. These relationships need to be right when Messiah comes.

In Islam, man's ultimate purpose is to worship Allah by obeying the teachings of the Koran and the traditions of Mohammed. For Muslims, the earthly life is a test to determine where the afterlife will be spent, whether in Paradise or in Hell. The final decision is Allah's alone and he can let some evil people go to Heaven and some good people go to Hell. The meaning of life is that it is a time of testing for a Muslim believer with no certainty that there will be any ultimate positive meaning.

I will deal with Christianity and why my life has meaning in a bit. First, some general comments about the meaning of meaning and the purpose of purpose as far as human life and religion are concerned. There is a difference even though much of philosophy and religion sees them as the same. When you pick up a hammer you know that it has a purpose. The design of it reflects that purpose. But nobody that holds a hammer looks at it and says, "What meaneth this hammer?" The hammer has no meaning; it only has a purpose.

Now, let's take it a step further and think about designer dresses. When a woman wears a dress, the purpose is to cover her body (or some of it these days). But if that woman wears a Dior, Armani, or Oscar de la Renta, that dress means envy and adulation for the one wearing it and it means glory and awe for the one who designed it. The dress only means something if it does more than fulfill a purpose. It means something if it adds value.

Let me give you some definitions of terms. First of all, by meaning I am not talking about the definition of the word in linguistic terms. Linguistically, the meaning of a word is the referent or thing signified by the word. A dog is a species of animals that has four legs, comes in all sizes and colors, sleeps on the sofa and hates cats. When you hear the word "dog," that is what you think of. That is what the word "dog" means. Do you see why we cannot use that definition of meaning to signify "meaning"? We have to give the word "meaning" a meaning.

For my purposes here, I use the word "meaning" as applied to life to mean "value." For my life to be meaningful, it has to have value, not value to me, but value to someone outside of me. The hammer has value only if it is valued by the one using it. The designer dress has value only if it is valued by the one wearing it. Life has value only if it brings something valuable to other people. In spite of what philosophers and psychologists say, I cannot make meaning for my life. I can set goals and achieve them. It will make me feel good. But that does not mean it adds value or meaning to other people's lives or to my life.

Everyone's biological life has meaning or value to themselves. But that biological life means existence. Remember the respondent who said, "The meaning of life is not being dead"? Human beings instinctively value their existence unless something convinces them they would be better off not existing. But we are not talking about biological existence here. We are talking about how that existence is lived out mentally, emotionally, spiritually as well as physically. Am I living in such a way that my life means something to somebody else? If it means something to another human being then my life has a limited meaning because I am going to die and the human being that values me is going to die. I have learned that a life of real meaning is a life that has permanent value. How did I find it?

In my quest for the meaning of my life, I could look to philosophical and scientific naturalism or to some form of supernaturalism. I immediately have to reject any kind of naturalism because it is an illusion. Even the naturalists believe in the supernatural when it comes to the existence of life. You can believe that life evolved from a lower life form but no matter how far back you go, you have to believe that somewhere in time dead matter became live cells. In the natural world, science has repeatedly demonstrated that life can come only from other life. It is called the scientific Law of Biogenesis; every living thing must come from a previous living thing. Spontaneous generation (life beginning spontaneously from non-living matter) is how it must have happened, but that is against the natural possibility. It is supernatural. And spontaneous generation is not a repeatable process so that it cannot be tested scientifically. So you see scientific naturalism is not scientific or natural. Why would I want to look there for the meaning of my life? I found the answer in the supernatural realm.

To find meaning for my life, I needed the answers to three life questions: "Where did my life come from?" "Why am I here?" and, "What is going to happen to me when I die?" (Where? Why? What?) Without meaningful answers that are true and existentially liveable, I could never be sure my life has any meaning. These answers must come from the supernatural realm because the natural realm through science or philosophy cannot answer questions of origin, purpose or final destination as pertains to life.

I have done the research and have found that the fullest explanation of the origin, purpose and destination of life is found in the first three chapters of the book of Genesis in the Bible. I found there a supernatural explanation that does not require any more faith to believe than does a naturalist philosophy and worldview. The Bible says, "The Lord God formed the man from the dust of the ground and breathed into his nostrils the breath of life, and the man became a living being." It also says that man was made in the image and likeness of God. Then it says that man sinned by disobeying God and when sin entered into human life the image of the likeness of God in man was marred and rendered dysfunctional. From this we learn why man is different from all other living creatures.

Unlike all other living things that do not have the image of God made into them, man can appreciate beauty, man can love, and man has a sense of morals that works through a conscience. Man is capable of rational thought, has an imagination and can change his environment through the use of machines and tools. All of these are God-like qualities, but because the image of God was marred by sin, these qualities no longer function as perfectly as they were created to do. Sinful man can appreciate ugliness, can hate and can be immoral with a misinformed conscience. Man can and does think irrationally at times and he can use machines and tools for evil purposes as well as good. According to the Bible, man has a free will and is more likely to use that free will for selfish ends than for benevolent ends. That, to me, pretty well explains how human life got here and why humans are the way they are. It is an explanation that is coherent, cohesive and liveable to the "Where" question.

The second question I must answer to find my meaning in life is "Why am I here?" "Why was I born?" "Does my life have a purpose?" Again, the Bible gives the answer. God said through the prophet Isaiah, "Bring my sons from afar and my daughters from the ends of the earth—everyone who is called by my name, whom I created for my glory, whom I formed and made." I am here to bring glory to God, my Creator, just as a designer dress brings glory to its designer-creator. How can I bring glory to God when he is perfect and sinless and I am not? If I was created in his image I must try my best to image him, but my image of him is messed up. Here is what convinced me and what sets Christianity apart from all other faiths and religions which require great effort on man's part. Man cannot lift himself up to God. God became a man so that he could lift man up to himself. The sin problem had to be dealt with and the divine image had to be made anew. This is what the Gospel of Jesus Christ promises and delivers to those who believe. By faith, I can be given a new life that desires to image God by living the way that glorifies him. This is not something that I have to strive to do, or a goal that I have to accomplish to have meaning. It is something that God does to those who believe in him and his Son, Jesus Christ. It is what happened to me on that seawall I told you about.

This is how A.W. Tozer expressed it in a prayer: "Oh God, I want to be right so that I can die right. Lord, I do not want my life extended if it would mean that I should cease to live right and fail in my mission to glorify you all my days!" My purpose in life is to bring glory to God today and throughout eternity, and when I do that, God values me as an eternal son. And in turn he brings value to my life by giving me a purpose in the spiritual realm and peace, blessings and contentment in the physical realm. This is the answer to the "why" question that is coherent, cohesive and liveable, and I am content with it.

The "What is going to happen to me when I die?" question was dealt with in Chapter 6, with the various options for an afterlife given. Either there is an afterlife or there is not and people cease to exist when they die. There is a lot of misinformation and disinformation out there about the afterlife in Christianity. Most folks would tell you that in Christian belief there is a judgment after we die and, as in Islam, that judgment determines whether we spend eternity in heaven or in hell, the determining factors being how good we were in life or whether or not our good deeds outnumbered our bad deeds. There is some truth in these statements but there is enough error to make you miss the essence of Christianity.

There is an eternal heaven and an eternal hell and there is a judgment after we die. But that judgment is not to determine where we will spend eternity; it has more to do with what heaven or hell will be like for us after we get there. All of us have made a decision about Jesus Christ and that decision means we have already been judged. If we do not believe in him, we are condemned to hell. If we do, we are saved for heaven. Death only makes the decision and accompanying judgment permanent. Where there is life there is hope of eternal life by believing in the Gospel of Christ. God has made this very clear in the words of Jesus Christ recorded in John 3:16-18:

> *16 For God so loved the world that he gave his one and only Son, that whoever believes in him shall not perish but have eternal life.*
>
> *17 For God did not send his Son into the world to condemn the world, but to save the world through him.*
>
> *18 Whoever believes in him is not condemned, but whoever does not believe stands condemned already because he has not believed in the name of God's one and only Son.*

That is Christianity 101. My life has meaning because it was created by God, for the purpose of bringing glory to God, with the reward of spending eternity with God. This is an answer to the "Where?" question that is coherent, cohesive and liveable.

Back in the 1970's I was active in a civic service and leadership training organization called the Jaycees. The Jaycees have a creed that I recited every meeting for many years the first line of which is, "Faith in God gives meaning and purpose to human life." Can you imagine a civic organization having a creed like that? Even though I recited that creed hundreds of times, it did not mean anything to me until I had that experience with God on the seawall. Since then, it has meant everything to me. My faith in God has given meaning and purpose to my life.

Maybe you are not convinced. Are you a betting man? Are you willing to bet the rest of your life in this world and your eternity in the afterlife that I am wrong? According to Pascal's Wager, that would not be a rational bet. Blaise Pascal was a seventeenth-century French philosopher, mathematician and physicist who charted new territory in probability theory and the formal use of decision theory. Pascal argued that belief in God is pragmatically justified in the long run because we have nothing to lose and everything to gain from holding that belief. If there is no God, there is no eternal judgment to fear. When life is over it is over, no matter how good or bad it was. But if there is a God...? Pascal was speaking of the God of the Bible, the God of Christianity. Here is the way his argument shaped up:

(1) If you believe in and live for God, and it is true that God does exist, you will be rewarded with eternal life in heaven—an infinite gain.

(2) If you do not believe in and live for God, and it is true that God does exist, you will be condemned to eternity in hell—an infinite loss.

(3) If you believe in and live for God, and it turns out that God does not exist, in the end you will have lost nothing because when you are gone you are gone—a finite loss.

(4) If you do not believe in God and God does not exist, you can live like you want to but in the end you lose everything because when you are gone you are gone—a finite loss.

Put simply, Pascal argued that the expected value of believing in God is vastly greater than that of not believing, since if you believe in God and commit yourself to a life of faith and obedience to God and it turns out to be true, then you win an enormous good (eternity in heaven). But if you believe and it turns out to be false, then you have lost nothing except a few years of living for yourself that disappears when you die. Therefore, the rational thing to do is believe in God.

Pascal's Wager cannot give you certainty that believing in and living for the God of the Bible is the way to find meaning for your life. But that certainty is promised by God if you believe and commit your life to him. Every believer is promised a seawall experience which will give meaning to life now and eternal life to come.

My perspective

I am writing this with the belief in *homo religiosus* (religious man) and that every worldview at its core is a religious worldview. Whether or not one believes in God affects all other worldview beliefs. Religion does not necessarily entail a belief in God or gods. A general definition of religion from one dictionary is: "a cause, principle, or system of beliefs held to with ardor and faith." Another dictionary defines religion as: "an organized collection of beliefs, cultural systems, and worldview that relates humanity to an order of existence." The religion of Buddhism has no God or gods. And you can see from these definitions that the worldview of atheism, humanism and scientific naturalism are religions and people living those worldviews are practicing a religion.

I see man as *homo religious* with a *sensus divinitatis* (awareness of divinity) who is *homo adorans* (worshipping man). Man naturally has a sense of something outside himself that is bigger or better than himself. Man has his God or gods, whether they are self-made or revealed. And man worships those gods. Look around you and see what people are giving themselves to.

In my view, man is also *homo religious* with a *sensus divinitatis* who is *homo adorans* and is *homo animalis* (man with a soul). Man is aware that there is an immaterial (Definition again! Not the immaterial that means unimportant, but the immaterial that means not made of matter.) element to his being. He has a mind, a will and he has emotions that are not physical. Whatever you believe about their source, you cannot take them out of your body and examine them.

I also believe that man is *homo religious* with a *sensus divinitatis* who is *homo adorans* and is *homo animalis* and is *corpus et spiritus* (body and spirit). Some theologians believe that the soul and the spirit of man are only different names for the immaterial part of man. The Bible says that man has a soul and that man has a spirit and that man is body, soul and spirit. That is what I believe because it fits reality. I know that I think and have emotions that are not physical. I know also that there is a spiritual realm. And I am not alone as there are many mystics and spiritualists in the world as well as animists. Can you sense whether someone has a good spirit or a bad spirit?

Finally, I believe that man is *homo religious* with a *sensus divinitatis* who is *homo adorans*, *homo animalis* and *corpus et spiritus* who is living *sub specie aeternitatis* (under the aspect of eternity). In British-speak, that's a lorry load of

Latin, but it does explain why my life has permanent meaning. Man is the only creature that can even imagine that there is life after death and according to some philosophers, if it can be imagined it cannot be impossible. You cannot imagine a red blue. But you can imagine a blue dog and that is possible with the right genetic modification.

I want to be the kind of old man whose life has meaning. How about you? Or are you lost in the meaning of life? Remember the Jaycee creed and Pascal's wager. And remember the words of Jesus Christ:

> *What good will it be for a man if he gains the whole world, yet forfeits his soul? Or what can a man give in exchange for his soul?*
>
> *Now this is eternal life: that they may know you, the only true God, and Jesus Christ, whom you have sent.*

Do you remember what Kurt Vonnegut said? Have you examined your life? Has it turned out to be a clunker so far? I examined my life and it was headed in that direction. So I have made some changes.

To be the kind of old man I want to be I must, first of all, be right with God. Then I want to be the right kind of person; one who tries to do right in all circumstances. Being that kind of person will bring contentment to my old age. That is my paradigm for 65 and beyond, and that is the kind of old man I want to be.

Epilogue

Prayer of an Anonymous Abbess
(c. 17th century)

Lord, thou knowest better than myself that I am growing older and will soon be old. Keep me from becoming too talkative, and especially from the unfortunate habit of thinking that I must say something on every subject and at every opportunity.

Release me from the idea that I must straighten out other peoples' affairs. With my immense treasure of experience and wisdom, it seems a pity not to let everybody partake of it. But thou knowest, Lord, that in the end I will need a few friends.

Keep me from the recital of endless details; give me wings to get to the point.

Grant me the patience to listen to the complaints of others; help me to endure them with charity. But seal my lips on my own aches and pains -- they increase with the increasing years and my inclination to recount them is also increasing.

I will not ask thee for improved memory, only for a little more humility and less self-assurance when my own memory doesn't agree with that of others. Teach me the glorious lesson that occasionally I may be wrong.

Keep me reasonably gentle. I do not have the ambition to become a saint -- it is so hard to live with some of them --

but a harsh old person is one of the devil's masterpieces.

Make me sympathetic without being sentimental, helpful but not bossy. Let me discover merits where I had not expected them and talents in people whom I had not thought to possess any. And, Lord, give me the grace to tell them so.

Amen

Is this the kind of old person you want to be? It is my prayer that it is and that you and I will be this kind of person. If it comes to pass, we will make the world a better place by our being here.

www.ingramcontent.com/pod-product-compliance
Lightning Source LLC
Chambersburg PA
CBHW021128300426

44113CB00006B/336